DANCE AND PLAY ACTIVITIES FOR THE ELEMENTARY GRADES

Suggestions for the Classroom Teacher

by

LOIS M. BAUER, M.A.
*Physical Education Instructor,
Public Schools, Schenectady, N. Y.*

and

BARBARA A. REED, M.A.
*Physical Education Instructor,
Public Schools, Schenectady, N. Y.*

VOLUME TWO
Grades Four to Six

1951
CHARTWELL HOUSE, INC.
NEW YORK   N. Y.

M. R. Fields, Editor for Health Education

PRINTED IN THE UNITED STATES OF AMERICA

FOREWORD

Teachers in the elementary schools have long recognized the gap between the tremendous supply of energy children have and the limited opportunities provided in school to direct some of that energy toward the growth process. In the past, the home assumed responsibility by informally prescribing or suggesting work and play. Gradually, because of the change in home life, the elementary school had to reinforce its program with dance and play activities designed to develop organic power, nerve stability, desirable personality traits and wholesome interests. Included in the activities were those of manual and musical correlation.

As the elementary school program enlarged to encompass not only the overt motor movements of the body but also the emotions, attitudes and interests, teachers believed themselves incompetent to participate in it. They felt that only specialists in the dance or physical education should assume the program responsibility. Yet this was contrary to the philosophy on which the elementary grades function: the classroom teacher is the center of program activities.

DANCE AND PLAY ACTIVITIES FOR THE ELEMENTARY GRADES shows the way out for the teacher. It contains experiences carefully adjusted to suit the physical and emotional level of the child at each grade. Equally valuable are

3

the accompanying scores or record sources. One need not be a specialist to interpret the descriptions of the games or dances. Diagrams further simplify the process.

The authors, with their experience as classroom teachers and as physical education and dance specialists, have clearly preceived the needs of the elementary school child and his teacher. The contents of the book as a whole are concise, yet complete. It should serve as an effective guide for the interested and concerned teacher in-training and in-service.

MOREY R. FIELDS

PREFACE

The form of physical education may change from grade to grade, but its importance remains the same at every stage of child development.

In this second volume, we suggest activities for grades four to six. We follow the system and plan sheets of the first volume, but there is no over lapping of information. All activities are different from those included in the first volume and the two books can be used independently of each other.

Consistently with the developing muscular and intellectual strength of these age groups, as well as with their growing social consciousness and taste for competition, emphasis was laid on group activity and sports.

The teacher should not feel that it is necessary to cover all the material included in the plan sheets or that the order by months has to be followed exactly. It might be more appropriate to teach an activity at another time than that listed in the book. At all times, these plans should be considered flexible and used as such.

Our purpose in writing this book was primarily to assist the elementary school teacher who had little or no physical education training. We feel that this book will make it easier for her to inspire the children to develop healthy bodies and minds through planned play. We should like the teacher to find pleasure in the use of our book, and if it assists her in bringing to the children all the enjoyment that can be derived from dance and play, we shall have achieved success.

L. M. B.

B. A. R.

ACKNOWLEDGEMENTS

We wish to express our thanks to Dr. Morey R. Fields and Dr. Carl A. Troester for their guidance and encouragement.

We are also indebted to Miss Mary Anna Quigley for supervising the typing of the manuscript; Miss Pauline Bascom and Miss Virginia French for the diagrams and stick figures; Miss Marilyn Fiddler for the art work; and Miss Betty Valenta who wrote the music scores.

Our appreciation is given to Miss Phyllis Bascom, Mr. Robert Campbell, Mr. Howard Westcott, and many teachers in the Schenectady Public Schools for their valuable suggestions.

CONTENTS

GENERAL SUGGESTIONS FOR CARRYING OUT AN ACTIVITY PROGRAM

1. Safety measures should be taught and strictly followed. Be sure that play areas are free from hazards. If it is impossible to remove some dangers, such as posts, adapt the program to suit the play space.

2. Sneakers or rubber-soled shoes should be a requirement for indoor activity. This is an important safety measure. If locker-room space is available, gym suits and sneakers should be worn by fifth- and sixth-grade pupils and stored in lockers.

3. Give special attention to light, heat, and ventilation of indoor play areas for comfort and to reduce hazards.

4. Have a storage place for equipment and see that it is not left lying around the play area. Leaders may take this responsibility.

5. Make the most of the activity period by having a definite plan in mind, equipment ready, and good class organization.

6. Balance your plan so that it will provide for total body development and not just for the development of one particular part of the body.

7. Activity should be carried on out-of-doors whenever possible. If the weather is cool, be sure that the activity is vigorous and that all children are included. On warm days, select quiet activities.

8. Give warm-up activity at the beginning of the period, particularly if the temperature in which you are conducting the activity is low.

9. When planning your program, consider the child's needs and interests. Correlate the program with classroom activities whenever possible.

10. Let the children have a part in choosing activities. Encourage them to bring in games and other activities which they have learned outside and have them teach these to the class.

11. Provide an opportunity for pupils to express creative ability, giving special attention to those who are reluctant to express themselves.

12. Develop pupil leadership but do not overlook the value of good followership either. Provide opportunities for leadership to as many as possible; not always for a select few.

13. Help develop consideration of the rights of others through courtesy, honesty, and "fair play." Activity programs offer opportunities to build such qualities.

14. Pupils should enjoy themselves and have fun when participating in an activity program.

GAMES

The *group game* is an important activity in the play experience of the elementary school child. Since these games require little organization and only a limited amount of skill, they are particularly popular in grades one to four. They seem to answer a child's need for expressing himself in play and to satisfy his desire for vigorous total body activity. There is also an opportunity for the child to learn to play with others and to respect the rights of his fellow players. For many, this is a new experience and it is an important part of social development.

Another type of game used in the elementary grades is the *team game*. It is usually introduced in the fourth grade. These games are not too highly organized at this level, but children begin to feel an interest in playing as a team rather than as individuals. Team play, in its true sense, is the highest form of organized play. Its value lies in the cooperation of the players working together toward a common end. Some outcomes of team games are the development of leadership, perseverance, a sense of responsibility, and fair play.

Teaching Suggestions

1. Have equipment ready. If possible, appoint leaders to help or give them full responsibility for equipment.

2. Make any explanation of a game short and to the point. It is helpful to demonstrate the activity.

3. Never let a game drag. When the children begin to lose interest, use a variation or change the game.

4. Use sparingly those games that provide activity for only a few. When they are used, change the players often so that all get a chance to participate.

5. If the activity is a vigorous one, and the pupils become tired, switch to a quiet game.

6. Use pupil leadership as much as possible; try to give all pupils an equal opportunity to assume responsibility and to direct activities themselves.

7. Permit the pupils to select their own games part of the time.

8. Teams should be of equal ability. This keeps the interest high and more enjoyment is derived.

9. Teach skills carefully and present them clearly; do not emphasize them to such a degree that the interest in the game is lost.

10. Be well informed on the playing rules and make sure they are carried out properly.

RELAYS

Relays have a natural appeal to elementary school children. They not only derive much enjoyment from the activity, but it also gives them an opportunity to release a great deal of physical and emotional energy in a wholesome manner. The natural response and enthusiasm exhibited by the children when participating in this form of activity is an indication of its place in the game program. Simple relays can be successfully introduced in the third grade.

Relays are easy to administer, but for good results, the teacher should give special attention to a few important playing rules and see that they are carried out. She should also familiarize herself with the methods used in various types of relays.

Teaching Suggestions

1. Explain the relay and then have one member of each team try the activity. Make corrections and suggestions for the benefit of the whole class. This should eliminate any misunderstanding regarding procedure.

2. Be sure that starting lines, turning points, and finish lines are clearly marked and definitely understood.

3. Do not have too many players on a team. Six to eight is a good choice.

4. Give a clear signal to start the relay and be sure that no

one crosses the starting line ahead of time. When the first player has completed his turn, he touches off the next player on the starting line and the game continues. The method of "touching off" may vary with the type of relay, but the principle is always the same.

5. Make sure that the games are played fairly. Disqualify any team whose members do not follow the starting-line rule or do not perform the activity correctly.

6. It is helpful to have a leader for each team who is responsible for the conduct of his team and sees that the members play fairly.

7. It is important to use some method to determine when a team is finished. One good way is to have each player in the line sit or squat down when he finishes his turn. It is then easy to check when the last player is through.

8. Be alert at all times, as the competition is keen and the finishes are often close. It is important to be accurate in naming the winning team.

9. If the teams have an uneven number of players, you may appoint the extra ones judges. However, be sure to change the judges after each relay so that all have a chance to participate.

10. Another method of taking care of an uneven number of players is to have one person on the team that is short of members run a second time.

11. Interest may be stimulated by letting pupils choose names for their teams such as: automobile makes, animals, colors, or well-known baseball or football teams. The choice of names will vary with the interest of the age group.

12. Assign points for first, second, and third place and, at the end of the period, add up the points of each team to determine which team places first for that period. This is especially good

for older age groups as it helps develop a greater team spirit.

13. If relays are used in the classroom, be sure that there are
no hazards. Have the children keep their feet out of the aisles.

14. Never allow players to run to a wall or any hard surface;
use turning points instead. These should be at safe distances
from walls or other hazards.

General Types of Formations Used in Relays

The Line Relay. The line-type relay is the simplest and
probably most often used. It consists of placing teams in single-
file formation behind a common starting line. The lines of players
should be at least four or five feet apart and more if space permits. Opposite each team a turning point is established. Never
have players run to a wall, fence, or other hard surface. The
distance of the turning point or turning line from the team will
depend on the type of relay and the available space.

Indian clubs or similar objects may be used as turning points.
If they are not available, a chalk mark may be drawn on the
floor. Still another method is to have a member from each team

take a position opposite each line of players, but be sure to change them for each relay, so that they have a chance to participate.

The method used in conducting this relay is to have the first player in each line go forward, around the turning point, or up to the turning line, and return to the starting line, touching off the next player who repeats the process. This continues until all have a turn.

The Shuttle Relay. This is similar to the line relay, except that each team is divided into two separate parts which are in parallel lines facing each other as shown in the diagram. The distance between the two starting lines depends on the relay being used and on the amount of available space.

The first player of each team on one side of the starting line runs and touches the first player of the other half of his team. This player then runs forward to the opposite line and touches off the second player on this half. This alternates back and forth until all have run. When a player has had his turn, he drops back to the end of his line so as to keep the playing space clear for the players who are participating.

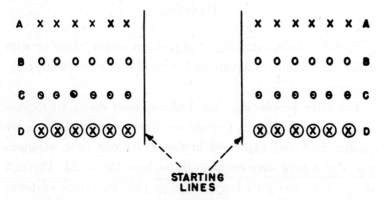

The Circle Relay. This relay is not as common as the line or shuttle type, but it can be used for variation.

Each team forms a circle of equal size. Allow sufficient space between circles for players to participate safely.

Number the players in each circle consecutively. At a starting signal, number one from each team runs clockwise around the outside of the circle and touches off number two. This continues until all have run. Other activities may be used instead of running.

It may be helpful to mark places on the floor where each player stands so that he will know his position after his turn. It will also help keep the circles equal in size.

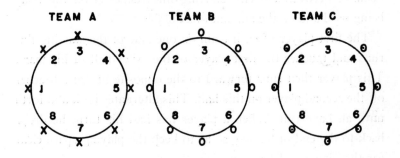

TEAM A   TEAM B   TEAM C

DANCING

Webster defines dancing: "to perform, either alone or with others, a rhythmic and patterned succession of movements, commonly to music."

Primitive people, e.g., the Indians, used dance to express various life experiences. Certain vocations and some legends are pantomimed and expressed in dance. At one time, religious and war dances were common throughout the world. Through dance, boys and girls learn about peoples, countries, customs, and traditions; at the same time they can enjoy the activity.

Since there is a feeling of freedom in dancing, it causes boys and girls to become more tolerant, courteous, and cooperative; therefore, dancing has a distinct social value. Our contribution through the teaching of dance is to instil, through a satisfying performance, a feeling of "what fun it is to dance and sing."

Singing games or song dances consist of a combination of words, music, and activity. They provide an easy way to teach rhythm and cadence, as they require little training or technical skill.

Teaching Suggestions

1. Have the children learn the tune and the words.
2. Fit the action to the song.
3. Victrola or piano accompaniment, where possible, adds to the ease and pleasure of the activity.

Folk Dances

These are colorful and gay traditional dances of many lands. The dances were handed down as a cultural heritage, and young and old participated. They were never meant to be watched.

Folk dances appeal through simple movement, good rhythm, and vigorous action. They encourage sociability and boys and girls learn to hold hands or arms without being self-conscious.

Teaching Suggestions

1. Be enthusiastic and patient.
2. Tell what you can about the dance—its nationality, origin, and the people who enjoy it.
3. Describe the native costume and, when possible, show pictures of it, or the costume itself.
4. Play the music; first for the class to listen, then for rhythm,

tempo, and phrasing. Let the children clap hands to the rhythm.

5. Decide whether to teach by the whole, part, or progressive method. This will depend on the ability of your class and the difficulty of the dance.

6. Explain and demonstrate any new steps to give the children a clear picture of what they are about to do.

7. Let the class try the new steps.

8. Put the dance together.

9. Your goal should be to have your class perform the dance smoothly and joyfully, and to have your dancers cooperate with various partners by repeating the dance several times without stopping.

Direction of Movement

1. Clockwise: The dancers move in the direction of the hands of the clock.

2. Counterclockwise: The dancers move in the direction opposite to the hands of the clock.

3. Line of Direction: The direction as indicated by the teacher as forward or backward, to the right or left.

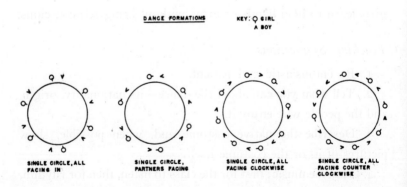

DANCE FORMATIONS   KEY: ○ GIRL
                               △ BOY

SINGLE CIRCLE, ALL FACING IN   SINGLE CIRCLE, PARTNERS FACING   SINGLE CIRCLE, ALL FACING CLOCKWISE   SINGLE CIRCLE, ALL FACING COUNTER CLOCKWISE

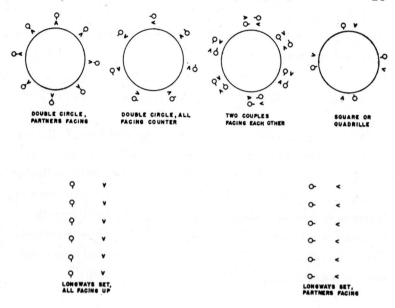

| DOUBLE CIRCLE, PARTNERS FACING | DOUBLE CIRCLE, ALL FACING COUNTER | TWO COUPLES FACING EACH OTHER | SQUARE OR QUADRILLE |

LONGWAYS SET, ALL FACING UP

LONGWAYS SET, PARTNERS FACING

Partner Changes

Moving to a new partner adds interest to the activity and improves the sociability of the dance group.

1. Form a single circle with partners facing, pass right shoulders and move forward one place to the new partner.

2. Form a double circle with partners facing.

(a) One circle stands still as the other circle moves one place to the right to a new partner.

(b) Both circles move one place to their own right to a new partner.

Facilities

1. Adequate floor space where possible.
2. Good ventilation.

3. A piano in good tune.

4. A victrola with a speed and volume control.

5. A folk dance music library.

SELF-TESTING ACTIVITIES

Self-testing activities are popular among children of all ages as they are fun to do and they present a challenge which encourages improvement in skill. In so doing, children build courage, perseverance, and self-confidence and satisfy an inherent desire for achievement. From a physical standpoint, these activities develop the child's strength, agility, and body control. They also offer an excellent opportunity to develop leadership, teach cooperation, and build a sense of responsibility.

Teaching Suggestions

1. If regulation gym suits are not required, it is suggested that girls bring play suits for these activities.

2. Many stunts listed in this book can be done without mats, but always use them if you have them. Eliminate an activity requiring mats if you do not have them. A substitute for a mat may be made by putting together two thicknesses of an old, heavy carpet.

3. Activities should be graded according to difficulty and should be adapted to the ability of the group.

4. Everyone should be able to achieve a certain amount of success.

5. Demonstrate the activity or have a capable member of the class do it.

6. Give helpful hints that may be useful to the pupil when performing the activity.

7. Instruct leaders how to assist properly and teach the importance of assisting to all members of the class. The activity should be a cooperative matter.

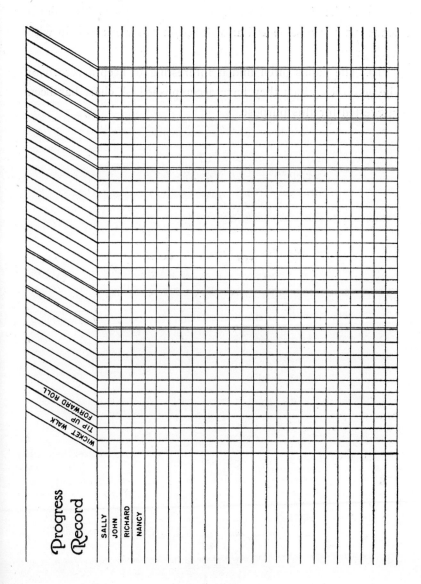

8. The class should be under your direct control; organization is important. Do not allow any "fooling" or "rough-housing" at any time.

9. If the class is large, divide it into groups and appoint a leader who is reliable and also skilled in this work to help with each group.

10. The pupils often find it interesting to keep a record of the activities which they have accomplished. A chart has been suggested for this purpose.

Grade Four

No unusual change in growth takes place as it is normally slow and steady at this time. Small muscles are developing and there is a higher degree of skill in perform-ance. Children have a variety of interests in activities, but particularly enjoy team sports, such as softball. They play hard and are apt to play strenuously, almost to the point of exhaustion.

The boys and girls are losing many of their childish character-istics. They show less dependence on others and can do more on their own initiative. The ability to concentrate is greater. There is considerable interest in perfecting skills. Often, activities they like are done over and over to improve them.

Competition on a group basis is stronger than before and the success of the group is of greater importance than individual accomplishment. Gang and club groups are beginning to be popular and exclusion of nonmembers is a noticeable feature. Play groups in class at school may include both boys and girls. When groups are organized by the children, these groups are usually composed of either all boys or all girls, depending on which sex does the initial selection.

SUGGESTED LESSON PLAN

September

Activities	Equipment	Section
GAMES		
Kick Ball	One rubber ball, four bases	16
Japanese Tag		15
Catch of Fish		4
Train Dodge Ball	One ball	28
DANCES		
Bummell Schottische	Victor Record 20448	42
Tretur		57
SELF-TESTING ACTIVITIES		
Heel Touch		72
Kangaroo Leap		74

October

Activities	Equipment	Section
GAMES		
Chain Tag		6
Team Dodge Ball	One ball	26
Line Soccer	One ball	18
Indian Club Snatch	One Indian club	14
DANCES		
Clap Dance	Victor Record 20450	43
Yankee Doodle	Victor Record 20166	59
SELF-TESTING ACTIVITIES		
Grapevine		71
Full Squat		70

November

Activities	Equipment	Section
GAMES		
Soccer Dodge Ball	One ball	23
Center Catch Ball	One ball	5
Team Soccer Dodge Ball	One ball	27
RELAYS		
Backward Walk Relay		30
Over and Under Relay	One ball for each team	39
DANCES		
Country Gardens	Victor Record 20802	44
Oh Susanna Circle	Folkraft Record F1017	50
SELF-TESTING ACTIVITIES		
Knee Dip		75
Walrus Walk		80

December

Activities	Equipment	Section
GAMES		
Sideline Dodge Ball	One ball	22
Numbers Change	One ball	19
Chariot Race Relay		31
DANCES		
Hopp Mor Annika	Victor Record 21618	46
Pop Goes the Weasel Square	Victor Record 20151	52
SELF-TESTING ACTIVITIES		
Knee Jump		76
Wheelbarrow		81
Forward Roll	A mat	67

January

Activities	Equipment	Section
GAMES		
Indian Club Guard	One ball and one Indian club	13
Circle Club Elimination	Three less Indian clubs or other objects than there are people in the group	7
RELAYS		
Object Balance Relay	One eraser or book for each team	38
Farmer and Crow Relay	Four bean bags or other objects for each team	35
DANCES		
Tantoli	Victor Record 20992	56
Swing the Corner Lady (Square)		55
SELF-TESTING ACTIVITIES		
Fish Hawk Dive		67
Rocking Chair		78
Backward Roll	A mat	62

February

Activities	Equipment	Section
GAMES		
King's Guard	One ball and one chair	17
Prisoner's Ball	One ball	21
Guard the Gold	Ten bean bags or other objects	10
RELAYS		
Double Squat Relay		34
Indian File Relay		36
DANCES		
Pinwheel Polka		51
Two Head Ladies Cross Over		58
SELF-TESTING ACTIVITIES		
Human Ball		73
Forward Roll with Crossed Legs	A mat	69
Back Rocker and Get-Up		61

March

Activities	Equipment	Section
GAMES		
Corner Spry	Four balls	8
Bombardment	Two balls and eight Indian clubs	3
RELAYS		
Couple Hop Relay		32
Crossed Legs Relay		33
DANCES		
Dutch Couple Dance		45
Irish Jig	Victor Record 21616	47
SELF-TESTING ACTIVITIES		
Bear Dance		63
Forward Roll Grasping Toes	A mat	68

April

Activities	Equipment	Section
GAMES		
Pirate's Treasure	One bean bag	20
Indian Club Bowl	One Indian club and one ball for each team	12
Softball Skills	Several softballs and a bat	25
RELAYS		
Pass and Squat Relay	One ball for each team	40
Kangaroo Relay	One ball for each team	37
DANCES		
Seven Jumps	Victor Record 21617	54
Modern Virginia Reel	Victor Record 20447	49
SELF-TESTING ACTIVITIES		
Forward and Backward Roll Combination	Mats	66
Coffee Grinder		64

May

Activities	Equipment	Section
GAMES		
Triangle Ball	One rubber ball, one bat, and two bases	29
Bat Ball	One bat, one rubber ball, and four bases	1
Body-Guard Tag		2
DANCES		
A Minuet	Victor Record 21938	1
Ribbon Dance	Victor Record 21619	53
SELF-TESTING ACTIVITIES		
Twister		79
Wicket Jump		82

June

Activities	Equipment	Section
GAMES		
Softball	One softball, one bat, and four bases	24
Farmer Tag		9
In-and-Out Race		11
DANCES		
Little Brown Jug	Folkraft Record G5003	48
SELF-TESTING ACTIVITIES		
Leg Twirl		77
Ankle Jump		60

GAMES

1. *Bat Ball*

Equipment: One softball bat, one rubber ball, and four bases. The ball should be larger than a softball, but not so large as to be cumbersome.

FORMATION

The game is played on a softball diamond. There are two teams, one is at bat and the other out in the field. Each team has a catcher, pitcher, first, second, third basemen, and fielders.

ACTION

This is played in the same manner as kick ball, except that the batter hits the ball with a softball bat. After the ball has been pitched and then hit by the batter, kick-ball rules apply.

NOTE

This is a good game for a lead-up to softball as it gives the children practice in hitting the ball with the bat.

2. *Body-Guard Tag*

FORMATION

The players are scattered about the playing area. There are three extra players, one is the "Chief" and the other two are "Guards." The Guards join inside hands and stand in front of the Chief.

ACTION

At a signal, the players attempt to tag the Chief without being tagged themselves by one of the Guards. Any player tagged by a Guard changes places with him. Any player who is able to tag the Chief becomes the Chief which is the important position to hold and one they are all working for. The Chief may move about the field as he wishes and the Guards move with him to protect him when necessary by tagging a player who gets too close. The two Guards must keep their inside hands clasped at all times and use only their free hands for tagging. Each time a player is tagged, the game is stopped temporarily until the players change places.

3. *Bombardment*

Equipment: Two balls; eight Indian clubs. This is only a suggested number of Indian clubs; more or less may be used.

FORMATION

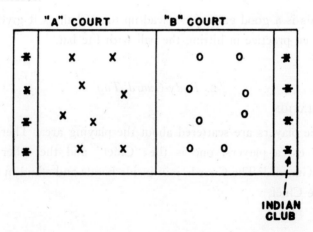

INDIAN
CLUB

A rectangular playing space is divided into two equal courts A and B, with a dividing line marked across the middle. In an area marked off across the end of each court, four Indian clubs are placed. There are two equal teams "A" and "B." Each takes its place in the respective court. The players scatter about the court and may move about freely as long as they remain in their own half of the area.

Action

One ball is given to team "A" and the other to team "B." At a signal, each throws the ball and attempts to knock the Indian clubs down behind the opposing team, at the same time trying to protect their own clubs. One point is scored for each club that is knocked down. The team having the greater number of points in a given playing time wins. Encourage passing the ball among the members of each team rather than having each person try for a direct hit.

4. *Catch of Fish*

Formation

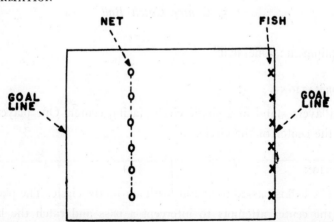

Goal lines are marked off at opposite ends of the playing space. There are two equal teams, one representing the "Fish" who stand on one goal line. The other team is the "Net" whose members join hands across the playing area about half to three-quarters of the way between the two goals.

ACTION

On a signal, the Fish attempt to reach the other goal line without being caught in the net. The players making the Net must keep their hands joined and try to catch as many Fish as possible by surrounding and closing in on them. The Fish can escape only by going around the ends and cannot go under the arms of the players. All Fish caught must join the Net team. The groups then change places and the Net becomes the fish and the Fish the Net. The game alternates in this manner until all on one side have been caught. If neither team is able to capture all of the others, the team having the greater number of players at the end of the playing time wins.

5. *Center Catch Ball*

Equipment: One ball.

FORMATION

Players stand in a single circle, facing center. One player is in the center of the circle.

ACTION

The ball is passed back and forth across the circle. The player in the center attempts to intercept a pass and catch the ball.

If he succeeds, he joins the players in the circle and the child who threw the ball takes his place in the center and play is resumed.

6. *Chain Tag*

FORMATION

One player is "It" and the others are scattered over the play area. Make all the boundary lines clear.

ACTION

"It" tags another player and that player joins hands with him. Together they tag another player who joins the line. This continues, but only the people on the ends are eligible to tag. If the chain or line is broken when tagging someone, it does not count. Any player who runs out of bounds to avoid being caught must join the line. The game is completed when all the players have joined the line or a definite number have been caught.

VARIATION

If the group is large and the playing area permits, two "Its" may be used instead of one. Thus, two chains would be made, and the chain having the greater number of players at the end of a predetermined period of time wins.

7. *Circle Club Elimination*

Equipment: Three less Indian clubs or other objects than there are people in the group. March music may be used; this is not essential, but adds interest to the game.

FORMATION

Single circle is formed, facing in the line of direction. The Indian clubs are placed in a circle equal distances apart just inside the circle formed by the group.

ACTION

The class marches around the circle to the music. When the music stops each player attempts to grasp a club. Since there are three less clubs than players, three will be without clubs and thus are eliminated from the game. Three clubs are now removed from the circle and the game continues. The players remaining in the circle after all clubs have been taken are the winners. If music is not available for marching, any other method for starting and stopping the group may be used.

8. *Corner Spry*

Equipment: Four balls.

FORMATION

In a rectangular playing area, a circle, about ten feet in diameter, is marked in the center. There are four equal teams and a Captain for each team is chosen. One team is in each corner of the playing area and the Captains take their places in the circle. Each Captain has a ball.

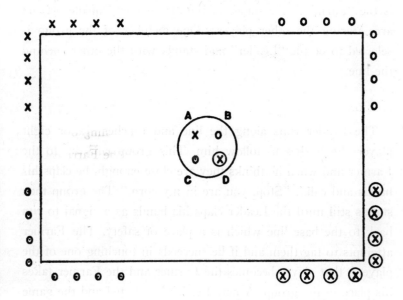

ACTION

At a signal, the Captain of each team starts passing the ball to each member of his team in succession. As each player receives the ball, he tosses it back and squats. When the Captain tosses the ball to the last player in the group he calls: "Corner spry" and runs to the head of the team as all members stand up. The last player runs to the circle and becomes Captain and repeats the performance. This is done until all members of the team have been Captain. The team whose original Captain first returns to the center wins.

9. *Farmer Tag*

FORMATION

A line across one end of the playing field is established for the base. All the players stand behind this line, except one who is the "Farmer." He stands at the opposite end of the playing area, facing the other players. One member of the group is selected to be the "Leader" and stands with the others behind the line.

ACTION

The Leader runs along the line and touches six or eight players he wishes to follow him. This group runs up to the Farmer and when he thinks they are close enough, he claps his hands and calls: "Stop, you are in my corn." The group then stands still until the Leader claps his hands as a signal to run back to the base line which is a place of safety. The Farmer attempts to tag them and if he succeeds in touching one of the players, that player becomes the Farmer and the Farmer takes his place in the group. A new Leader is selected and the game is started again. If the Farmer does not catch anyone, he continues to be the Farmer.

VARIATION

When a Farmer tags a player, this player is out of the game. A new Farmer and Leader are chosen and the original Farmer and Leader take their places behind the base line.

10. *Guard the Gold*

Equipment: Ten bean bags, or other objects.

FORMATION

A rectangular playing space is marked off, with a line drawn across the middle. A goal is marked at each end and five bean bags are placed in each goal. The bean bags represent the bags of gold. The players are divided into two equal teams. Each is scattered in its own half of the field. Three players from each team are appointed guards and stand ten feet in front of their goal. They do not go nearer the goal area except to tag someone.

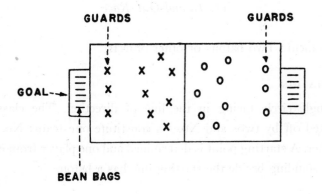

ACTION

Members of each team attempt to take all the bags of gold from the opponent's goal and bring them to their own goal. As soon as a player crosses the middle line, he may be tagged by a member of the opposite team. If, however, he is able to reach the goal without being tagged, he may take one of the bags of gold and return it to his goal without being tagged. If a player is tagged while attempting to obtain the gold, he becomes a prisoner and remains behind the opponent's goal line until one team has captured all the bags of gold. The team which first captures all the bags of gold wins. All the prisoners are then released and the game is restarted.

VARIATION

A prisoner may be rescued by a player of his team if he is able to reach the goal area without being tagged. He then returns to safety with his rescuer. When this method is used no gold may be taken from the area as long as there are prisoners. They must all be rescued first.

11. *In-and-Out Race*

Equipment: Two batons or other objects.

FORMATION

Single circle facing in the line of direction. The class is counted off by twos and No. 1's constitute one team; No. 2's another. A starting point is determined and one player from each team standing beside the starting line has a baton.

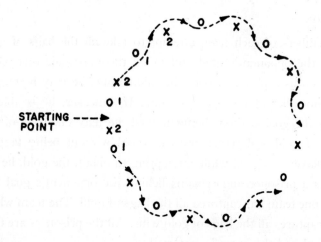

ACTION

At a signal, both players run in opposite directions around the circle going to the rear of the first player, in front of the second, and to the rear of the third. They continue to run in and out until they reach the starting line. Then the first player hands the baton to the next one on his team who repeats the process. This continues until all players have run and the team finishing first wins. The people in the circle should stand in their places and not interfere with the runner. When a runner has had his turn he returns to his place.

12. Indian Club Bowl

Equipment: One Indian club and one ball for each team.

FORMATION

Equal teams stand in single lines behind a starting line. One Indian club is placed about twelve feet in front of each line. A Leader is appointed for each team and after he has his turn he acts as pin boy and scorer for his team. Each team has a ball.

ACTION

The first player in each line rolls the ball and attempts to knock over the Indian club. If he succeeds he scores a point for his team. The next player in line then takes his turn and the game continues until all have had a turn at knocking over the club. If anyone steps over the starting line, the score does not count. The team having the highest score wins.

13. Indian Club Guard

Equipment: One ball; one Indian club.

FORMATION

Children form single circle, facing center. The Indian club is placed in the center of the circle and one player is chosen to stand in the center to guard the club.

ACTION

The players in the circle attempt to knock over the club by throwing the ball at it. The guard in the center may protect the club by batting the ball away, blocking it with his body or kicking it. If player succeeds in knocking over the club, he becomes the new guard and the original guard takes his place in the circle. Play is then resumed.

VARIATION

1. Two balls may be used instead of one.

2. Two Indian clubs and one ball may be used.

3. Three Indian clubs may be arranged to form a triangle in the center of the circle with one guard. The ball is kicked by the players forming the circle instead of being thrown. The players may recover the ball, both outside and inside the circle, but may only kick it at the clubs from their respective positions in the circle. The guard in the center may only use his feet to protect the clubs. Any player who succeeds in knocking over any of the clubs changes places with the guard and play is resumed.

14. *Indian Club Snatch*

Equipment: One Indian club.

FORMATION

There are two equal teams on parallel lines, facing each other. These lines are from fifteen to twenty feet apart. One Indian club is placed in the center of the area midway between the two lines. The players on each team are numbered consecutively, starting at opposite ends.

```
  1   2   3   4   5   6   7   8
  X   X   X   X   X   X   X   X  _____

                  ✻ INDIAN CLUB

  _____  O   O   O   O   O   O   O   O
          8   7   6   5   4   3   2   1
```

ACTION

The instructor calls out a number that has been assigned. Both children who have that number run forward, trying to snatch the club and bring it back across their own line without being tagged by the opposite player. If each of them is successful, he scores a point for his team. Each player then returns to his place. Another number is called and the game continues. The team scoring more points wins. If two players should grasp the club at the same time, it is considered a draw and neither team scores a point.

15. *Japanese Tag*

FORMATION

Players are scattered about the playing area. One player is "It."

ACTION

"It" attempts to tag one of the players and when he succeeds, the child caught becomes "It," but he must keep his left hand on the spot where he was tagged and use his right hand to tag. The object is to try and tag a player in an awkward place, thus making it difficult for him to run.

16. *Kick Ball*

Equipment: One rubber ball, four bases.

FORMATION

A softball diamond is used with bases thirty feet apart. There are two equal teams. One takes its place in the field and the other

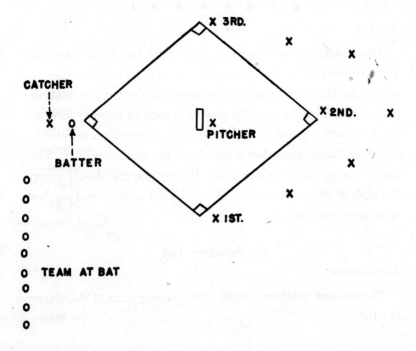

is up at bat. Each team consists of a catcher, pitcher, first, second, and third basemen, one or two shortstops, and three fielders (right, left, and center).

ACTION

The pitcher rolls the ball to the batter who kicks it forward into the playing area. If it is a "Fair Hit Ball" he runs to first base or as many bases as he can reach without being put out. The runner must touch each base in order.

The batter is out if

1. the fielder touches the base with any part of his body while the ball is held in his hands before the runner reaches the base.
2. he is hit by a thrown ball by any of the players on the opposite team while running his bases.
3. any fly ball is caught.
4. four foul balls are hit.
5. he runs more than three feet outside the base line to avoid being tagged.

Teams change sides when there are three outs. Each team must have an equal number of times at bat to complete a game. Usually a definite number of innings are decided on before starting a game.

NOTE

Fly Ball is a ball kicked by the batter that is caught by any of the players on the opposite team before it touches the ground.

Fair Hit Ball is a ball that is kicked and remains in the field of play between home and first and home and third. If the ball is hit in the outfield and rolls out of the field of play, it is considered a Fair Ball.

Foul Ball is a kicked ball that lands out of fair territory or that rolls out of fair territory between home and first or home and third.

17. *King's Guard*

Equipment: One ball and one chair.

FORMATION

Players form single circle, facing center. A chair is placed in the center of the circle to represent the "King's Throne." One player is chosen to be the "King" and takes his place in the chair. Two other players are selected to be "Guards" and stand near the King. The players forming the circle have a ball.

ACTION

The players throw the ball and attempt to hit the King. It is the duty of the two Guards to protect the King. They may use their hands, feet, or body in any way to block the ball to keep it from hitting him. When a player succeeds in hitting the King, he becomes King and the King takes his place in the circle. The new King chooses two new Guards and the others return to the circle. The game then continues.

VARIATION

Two balls may be used instead of one.

18. *Line Soccer*

Equipment: One ball.

FORMATION

Two equal teams are formed, with a Captain for each team. The players of each team stand side by side, with hands joined in a single line. The two teams face each other about twenty to thirty feet apart. The ball is placed halfway between the two lines in the center of the area.

ACTION

At a signal, the two Captains come forward and kick the ball. The players in the lines act as guards and may move about anywhere as long as they keep their hands joined. A point is scored if either the Captains or guards succeed in kicking the ball over or through the opposite line. The ball may only be touched with the feet. If a player uses his hands he is out of the game and a point is scored for the other team. The team scoring more points during the playing time wins. Choose new Captains after a point is scored.

19. *Numbers Change*

Equipment: One ball.

FORMATION

Single circle is formed, facing center. One extra player is "It" and stands in the center of the circle with a ball. The players forming the circle are numbered consecutively.

ACTION

"It" calls any two numbers and the children whose numbers are called exchange places. As soon as the numbers are called,

"It" throws the ball to anyone in the circle. The player receiving the ball returns it immediately to "It" who then attempts to hit one of the two players exchanging places. If he succeeds in hitting a player before he reaches his new place, that player becomes "It." If he does not hit anyone, he remains "It" and the game continues.

20. *Pirate's Treasure*

Equipment: One bean bag.

FORMATION

A square playing area is marked out and a circle, six feet in diameter, is drawn in the center to represent an "Island." A bean bag or other object is placed in the circle to represent the "Treasure." One player is the "Pirate." He takes his place near the Island to guard the Treasure. The other players stand at intervals outside the square.

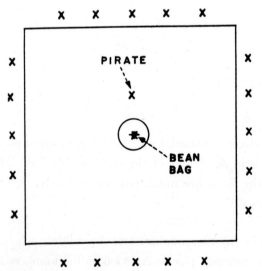

ACTION

A signal is given at which the players run into the square and attempt to secure the Treasure. If a player is able to capture the Treasure and return to his place on the sideline before being tagged by the Pirate he becomes the new Pirate and the original Pirate takes his place on the side. If, however, he is tagged while attempting to bring back the Treasure he is out of the game until there is a new Pirate. In guarding the Treasure, the Pirate must not run across the Island until the Treasure has been captured. The Pirate who is able to eliminate the greatest number of players during the playing time is the winner.

21. *Prisoners' Ball*

Equipment: One ball.

FORMATION

A rectangular playing space is divided in three courts. The center court is neutral and is about four yards wide. Each team has an area at the end for prisoners. There are two equal teams, "Red" and "Blue." The players on each team are numbered.

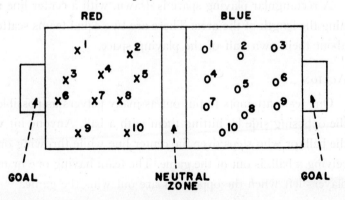

ACTION

Play is started by having one member of the Red team call a member of the Blue team by number and the player who calls the number throws the ball to the opponents. Any member of the Blue team may catch the ball. If the ball is dropped, the person whose number was called becomes a prisoner and must go to the opponents' goal area. Play is resumed by having the Blue team throw the ball and call a number. Play continues until one whole team is captured. A team has the privilege of returning a prisoner to play rather than putting out an opponent. This is done by calling the number of one of the prisoners before the ball is thrown. If the ball is dropped, the prisoner returns to play with his team. If at any time the ball falls in neutral territory or is thrown out of bounds, it does not count and it is given to the opposite side.

22. *Sideline Dodge Ball*

Equipment: One ball.

FORMATION

A rectangular playing space is drawn, with a center line running the length of the area. There are two equal teams scattered about their own half of the playing space.

ACTION

One team attempts to put out as many players as possible on the opposing side by hitting them with a ball. Anyone hit with the ball, or who steps over the center line while throwing or receiving a ball, is out of the game. The team having one or more players left when the opponents are out wins the game.

VARIATION

Two balls may be used instead of one if the playing area is adequate.

23. *Soccer Dodge Ball*

Equipment: One ball. It does not have to be a soccer ball. A rubber playground ball may be used.

FORMATION

Players form single circle, facing center. Two or three players go inside the circle.

ACTION

The players forming the circle kick the ball back and forth across the circle attempting to hit one of the players in the center who may run, dodge, or jump to avoid being hit. The ball may be advanced with any part of the body except the hands and arms. If a player does use his hands, he is eliminated from the game. When one of the players inside the circle is hit with the ball, he exchanges places with the player who hits him and the game continues. If the ball goes outside the circle or stops inside, the nearest player recovers it by dribbling (tapping the ball with his feet) and returns to his place in the circle. Any player on the inside of the circle who steps outside to avoid being hit is out of the game and another player is chosen to take his place.

VARIATION

Two balls may be used instead of one. More players may be chosen to go in the center if the class is large and the playing space is adequate.

24. *Softball*

Equipment: One softball, one bat, and four bases.

FORMATION

The playing area is a thirty-five foot softball diamond, with first, second, and third base, home plate, and a pitcher's box. There are nine players on each team as follows: catcher, pitcher, first, second and third basemen, one shortstop, and three fielders; right, left, and center. One team is at bat and the members of the other take their positions in the field.

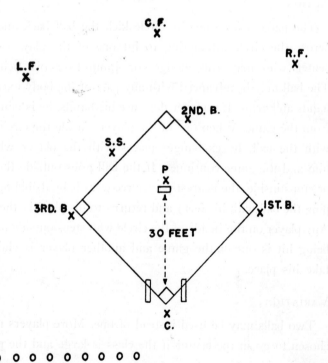

ACTION

The team at bat attempts to score while the team in the field tries to put it out according to specified rules. A team is at bat until it has three outs and then it changes with the players in the field. Runs are scored by the batter hitting a pitched ball and touching first, second, third bases, and home plate in that order without being put out. The team having more runs after an equal number of times at bat wins.

The following rules are summarized briefly for the game. See official rule book for a complete set of rules.

1. Game. A regulation game consists of seven innings, but more or less may be played if agreed upon. An inning is completed when each team has had a turn at bat.

2. Batting order. The order in which players take their turn at bat is determined before the game starts and must be followed. When a team resumes its turn at bat after being in the field, it must continue its batting order where it was left off when the last out was made.

3. Pitching. The underhand pitch is used and the pitcher must stand in his pitching box when the pitch is made.

4. Fair Ball. Any legally batted ball that:

a. Comes to rest on fair territory between home and first and home and third.

b. Strikes into foul territory, but rolls on to fair ground and settles there.

c. Strikes on fair territory in the outfield and then rolls foul.

5. Foul Ball. A legally batted ball that strikes out of fair territory or rolls out of fair territory between home and first base or home and third base.

6. Strike. a. When a legally pitched ball passes over home plate between the knees and shoulders of the batter and is not hit by the batter.

b. When the batter swings and misses any legally pitched ball.

c. When the batter hits a foul ball that is not caught by a fielder. The first two of these are called strikes.

d. When the batter hits a foul tip that is held by the catcher.

7. Foul tip. a. A legally batted ball that goes directly and sharply off the bat and is caught by the catcher. If not caught it is simply a foul hit.

b. Any foul tip caught is a strike regardless of whether it is first, second, or third strike.

c. A foul-hit ball which rises higher than the batter's head shall not be considered a foul tip under this rule.

8. Batter is out if he: a. Makes three strikes.

b. Hits a fair or foul ball which is caught by a fielder before it touches the ground.

c. Hits a foul tip which is legally caught on the third strike.

d. Steps from one batter's box to the other when a pitcher is ready to deliver the ball.

e. Attempts to hinder the catcher from fielding the ball.

f. Bats out of order, provided the error has been discovered before there has been a pitch to another batter.

9. Batter becomes a base runner: a. After a fair hit ball that has not been caught before touching the ground.

b. After four balls have been called by the umpire.

c. If the catcher interferes or prevents the batter from striking a pitched ball.

10. Base runner is out if he: a. Hits a fair ball and is touched with the ball by a fielder before touching first base or the ball is legally held by a fielder on first base before the runner touches first base.

b. Runs three feet outside of base line to avoid being tagged by a fielder.

c. Fails to return to base on fly ball caught before the base man secures ball.

d. Is tagged while off base, except in case of a foul ball.

e. Is hit by a fair hit ball before it has been touched by a fielder.

SUGGESTED SAFETY MEASURES

a. Call a batter out if he throws his bat.

b. See that the players waiting for their turn at bat stay a safe distance from the batter.

25. Softball Skills

CATCHING

1. Use both hands in a cupped position, fingers should not be stiff.

2. Let the hands "give" with the ball.

3. If the ball is above the waist, point the fingers up, thumbs together.

4. If the ball is below the waist, point fingers down, little fingers together.

5. Close fingers firmly around the ball as it comes in contact with the hand.

UNDERHAND PITCH

1. Hold the ball in the palm of the hand with the palm up.

2. The weight is on the right foot.

3. Swing the right arm backward. Then swing the right arm forward, keeping it close to the body. At the same time, take a long step forward with the left foot.

4. Release the ball about hip high at the end of the swing and follow through.

OVERHAND THROW

1. Hold the ball in the palm of the hand with the palm down. Place the thumb on the left, the first, and second fingers on the top, and the fourth and little finger on the right.

2. Swing the arm backward, keeping the elbow bent and the ball at shoulder level.

3. The weight is on the right foot and the left shoulder turned forward.

4. Swing the right arm up, over, and forward, releasing the ball at the end of the arm swing. At the same time, step forward with the left foot.

5. Follow through with the arm and body.

BATTING

1. Stand facing the plate in a stride position.

2. Hold the bat in both hands almost together at the end of the bat, with the right hand high.

3. Hold the bat near the right shoulder, but not resting on it and with the left elbow almost shoulder high and parallel to the ground.

4. Keep the eyes on the pitcher and the ball as soon as it is released.

5. Shift the weight to the right foot in preparation for swinging. Swing the bat forward and parallel to the ground, and transfer the weight from the right to the left foot. Follow through with the arms and the body.

6. Do not throw the bat at the end of swing; drop it.

FIELDING A GROUND BALL

1. The fielder should try to get his body in the path of the ball.

2. As the ball approaches, the player's knees are bent so as to enable him to reach the ball. The player is in stride position, one foot slightly in advance of the other.

3. The hands are held close together, fingers pointing down and palms facing the ball. "Give" with the ball as you receive it.

4. Straighten the body and throw it as soon as possible.

FIELDING A FLY BALL

1. It is best to receive it in front of the chest.

2. The hands are close together and are in a cupped position with palms up.

3. As the ball reaches the hands, "give" with it and close fingers around it.

4. Throw the ball to the proper place as soon as possible.

26. *Team Dodge Ball*

Equipment: One ball.

FORMATION

There are two equal teams. One team forms a single circle, facing center, around the outside of a circle marked on the playing area. The other team is scattered inside the circle. The team on the outside has the ball.

ACTION

The players on the outside of the circle throw the ball and attempt to hit as many players in the circle as possible in a given length of time. They score one point for their team for each person they hit. The person hit must go outside the circle and is temporarily out of the game. When time is up, the teams change places and the game is started again. The team hitting the greater number of players in a given time wins the game. Whenever a player goes inside the circle to recover the ball, he must return to his place in the circle before he can throw it. The players on the inside run, dodge, jump, or stoop to avoid being hit by the ball.

VARIATION

Instead of playing for a given length of time, a team continues to play until all players in the circle have been hit and eliminated from the game. The instructor keeps an account of the time it takes to put all the members of a team out. The teams change places and the process is repeated. The team taking less time to put the other team out wins.

27. *Team Soccer Dodge Ball*

This is similar to soccer dodge ball, except that the class is divided into two equal teams with one team inside the circle and the other out. When a player in the center is hit by the ball, he is eliminated from the game. The teams change places at the end of a given length of time and the side eliminating the greater number of players wins.

28. *Train Dodge Ball*

Equipment: One ball.

FORMATION

Children form single circle, facing center. Three or four players go in the center and form a train by linking their arms around the waist of the one in front of them. The one in front represents the "Engine," the one in the rear is the "Caboose," and the other players are the "Passenger Cars."

ACTION

The players forming the circle have a ball. They throw the ball, attempting to hit the last player or Caboose. The Engine may try to protect the Caboose by batting the ball with his hands or kicking it away with his feet. He also tries to maneuver the group to keep out of the path of the ball. The Passenger Cars and Caboose must not touch the ball and must keep their hands clasped around the one in front of them.

If a player succeeds in hitting the Caboose of the train, he takes the place of the Engine and all move back to position. The last player goes out of the center of the circle and joins the other players. The game continues.

VARIATION

Use two balls instead of one.

29. *Triangle Ball*

Equipment: One rubber ball, a little larger than a regulation softball, one softball bat, and two bases. A softball may be used in place of the rubber ball.

Formation

The playing area is a softball diamond, but only home, first base, and pitcher's box should be used. There are two equal teams, one is at bat and the other is scattered about the field. One of the field players is designated to be the pitcher and another the catcher.

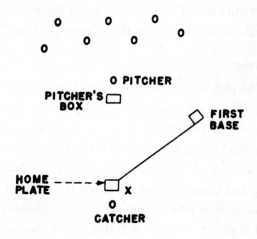

Action

The pitcher throws or pitches the ball to the batter who attempts to hit it with the bat. If he succeeds, he runs to first

base and back home scoring a run for his team. The batter may run on any kind of hit (fair or foul). The fielders try to get the ball as soon as it is hit and throw it to the pitcher who immediately throws it to the catcher. The catcher then touches home plate with the ball. If he does this before the runner returns home, the runner is out. A runner is also out if he has had three strikes or if a fielder catches a batted ball before it touches the ground. The run must be continuous from home to first and back. When a team has three outs they change places. The team having the greater number of runs after an even number of times at bat wins.

VARIATION

A first baseman may be used in addition to the pitcher and catcher. He may put the runner out at first if he touches first base with the ball before the runner gets there.

NOTE

This is a good softball lead-up game as it teaches many of the skills used in softball.

RELAYS

30. *Backward Walk Relay*

Teams are in single lines behind a starting line. The first player in each line walks backward to a turning line, runs around and returns to place, touching off the next player.

31. *Chariot Race Relay*

Teams are in single lines behind a starting line. Each team divides into groups of three, with two players standing in front and one behind to represent a "Chariot." The two players in front join inside hands with each other and outside hands with the player standing behind. At a signal, the first Chariot in each line runs forward to a turning line then returns to place, touching off the next Chariot in line. This continues until all Chariots in each team have had a turn.

32. *Couple Hop Relay*

An even number of players on each team are in single lines behind a starting line.

Each team pairs off into couples. The first two players in each line stand side by side and place the inside arms around each other's waist. They bend the knees of their outside legs, and grasp their ankles with their outside hands. In this position, they hop forward to a turning line. When they reach the line, they release their ankles, join inside hands, and run back to place touching off the next couple.

33. *Crossed Legs Relay*

Teams are in single lines behind a starting line. The first player in each line crosses his right leg over his left and walks forward to a turning line. On the turning line, the player changes the position of his legs, crossing left over right, and returns to place. The next player in line does the same.

34. *Double Squat Relay*

Players of each team squat two or three feet apart in single lines. The first player in each line gets up and runs around the back of his line and then forward around the front returning to his own place. Before the player squats down in line again, he places his hands on the hips and bends his knees to a squat position twice in rapid succession. When that player is down, the next one in line repeats the process. Another stunt or activity may be substituted for the squat position.

35. *Farmer and Crow Relay*

An even number of players on each team are in single lines behind a starting line. Small circles in a row are drawn several feet apart in front of each team. The first player in each line is the "Farmer," the second the "Crow," the third the Farmer, and so forth. Four bean bags to represent "Seeds" are placed in front of each line.

The first Farmer in each line picks up the four bean bags, runs forward, and plants his Seeds, dropping one bean bag on each circle. He then returns to the starting line and touches off the next player, the Crow. The Crow hops forward on his right foot to the place where the last Seed is planted, taking his weight on his left foot and hopping back to place picking up all the Seeds on his way. The Seeds are placed on the starting line and the next Farmer picks them up and plants them. This continues until all have had a turn.

36. *Indian File Relay*

Teams are in single lines behind a starting line. Each team is divided into three or four groups, depending on the number in line. The players in each group place their arms about the waist of the one in front. At a signal, the first group in each line runs forward to a turning line and returns to place touching off the next group. If the linked arms of the players break, they must stop and rejoin them before continuing.

37. *Kangaroo Relay*

Teams are in single lines behind a starting line. The first player in each line has a ball which he places between his knees. At a signal, he jumps forward to a turning line, keeping the ball between his knees. He must not touch the ball with his hands. If he drops it, he must replace it and continue jumping from the spot where he lost it. When the player reaches the turning line, he takes the ball in his hands, runs back to place and hands the ball to the next player as the game continues.

38. *Object Balance Relay*

Teams are in single lines behind a starting line. The first player in each line has a flat object, such as a book or an eraser, and places it on his head. He walks forward to a turning line, sits down, then gets up, and returns to place without losing the object from his head or touching it with his hands. The second player takes the object from the first player's head, places it on his own and repeats the process. If the object falls off, the player must stop and replace it before continuing.

39. *Over and Under Relay*

Teams are in single lines behind a starting line. A turning line is established twenty feet in front of each team. The first player in each line has a ball. At a signal, he passes the ball back over his head to the second player who takes it and passes it between his legs to a third player. The ball is passed alternating over and under until the last person in line receives it. He takes the ball and runs forward to the turning line and then back to the front of his line. This player now passes the ball back over his head and the same procedure is followed as the first time. This continues until all players are back in their original places.

40. *Pass and Squat Relay*

Teams are in single lines behind a starting line. One player from each team is chosen Captain. He takes his place ten feet in front of his team facing it. The Captain of each team has a ball which he passes to the first player in his line who catches it and returns it to the Captain. The first player then quickly squats down. The Captain now throws the ball to the second player who does the same. Play continues until all have had a turn. The team with all players in a squatting position first wins.

DANCES

41. *A Minuet*
(French)

Record:
Victor 21938

BASIC STEPS

Walk; step and point.

FORMATION

Sets of six couples in parallel lines facing front are formed. The girl is on the right of the boy. The inside hands are joined and held shoulder high. The boy puts the outside hand on his hip and the girl holds her skirt with the outside hand.

DANCE

Part 1

Measures

1-6   Three minuet steps* are taken starting on the right foot.

7-8   Partners face and boys bow, girls make a low curtsey.

1-8   Repeated: Dancers face in the opposite direction and repeat the above steps.

Part 2

9   Partners face, join right hands, and hold them

* The minuet step is: Point right toe forward. Step forward with the right foot, step forward with the left foot, step forward again on the right foot. Point the left toe and tap the left toe twice.

high. Both step forward on the right foot, draw the left foot to the right, and rise on the toes, then lower the heels.

10 They step back on the left foot, draw the right foot back to the left, and bow. The right hands are joined.

11-12 With right hands still joined, partners change places with three walking steps. Drop hands and bow.

13-16 Dancers join right hands and take three walking steps back to their own place.

Part 3

9-10 Partners are facing. Partners 1, 3, and 5 take one minuet step in place. Right hands are joined and held high. The other partners are standing still.

11-14 Partners 1, 3, and 5 take two minuet steps and turn around each other. Partners 2, 4, and 6 stand still.

15-16 All dancers bow.

9-14 Partners 2, 4, and 6 dance part 3 as couples 1, 3, and 5 stand still.

15-16 All dancers bow.

1-8 All repeat part 1.

42. *Bummell Schottische*
(German)

Record:
Victor-20448

BASIC STEPS

Slide; running schottische.

FORMATION

Double circle is formed, facing the line of direction; left side turned toward the center of the circle. Inside hands are joined, the girl being on the outside.

DANCE

Measures

1   Touch your right heel forward and bend the body back; touch the right toe beside the left foot and bend your body forward.

2   Slide the right foot to the side, close with the left, and slide right.

3-4 Repeat 1 and 2, starting left.

5-6 Repeat 1 and 2.

7   Spin around once in place, turning away from your partner.

8   Stamp in place left, right, left.

9-14 Take six running schottische steps forward, starting with the right foot.

15   Take four running steps, turning in place to right; step right, left, right, left.

16   Do three stamps; right, left, right.

Repeat all.

43. *Clap Dance* (Klappdans)
(Swedish)

Record:
Victor-20450

BASIC STEP

Polka.

FORMATION

Double circle is formed, facing the line of direction, girl on the outside.

DANCE

Measures

1-4   Beginning with the outside foot, take three polka steps forward and follow with three stamps in place.

5-8   Repeat the three polka steps, but face in opposite direction on the stamps.

1-8   Repeat the same step in the new direction, but face partner on the last three stamps.

9   Bow to partner.

10   Clap both hands with partner three times.

11-12   Repeat 9-10.

13   Clap own hands once, then clap partner's right hand, using own right hand.

14   Clap own hands and then partner's left hand.

15   Clap own hands and then partner's right hand.

16   Do three stamps in place, turning to face in the line of direction.

Repeat all.

44. *Country Gardens*

Record:
Victor-20802

BASIC STEPS

Step-hop; running schottische.

FORMATION

Couples stand in a single circle, facing center, all hands joined.

DANCE

Measures

1-4   Take four running schottische steps, moving to the right.

1-4   Repeat moving to the left.

5-8   Hand on hips, girls take four step-hops toward the center of the circle and four step-hops moving back to place.

9-16   Boys repeat the same.

13-16   Hook right elbows with partner and step-hop, turning in circle to the right.

13-16   Repeat, hooking left elbows.

Repeat all.

45. *Dutch Couple Dance*
(Dutch)

BASIC STEPS

Dutch step; step-hop; hop-waltz.

FORMATION

Dancers form double circle, facing in the line of direction, with inside hands joined; girl on the outside.

DANCE

Counts

9   Take three dutch steps forward, step on the outside foot, count 1, brush the other foot across, count 2, and hop on the outside foot, count 3.

3   Take three stamps in place: left, right, left.

9   Repeat first nine counts.

3   Both turn left with three stamps to face in the opposite direction. Stamp left, right, left.

24   Repeat the first twenty-four counts, but turn and face your partner on the last three stamps.

12   Place your hands on the hips and take four step-hops away from your partner. Girl steps back right and boy left.

12   Take four step-hops toward partner.

18   Take six hop-waltz steps.

6   Take four stamps in place, turning to face in the line of direction. Hold the last count in preparation for repeating the dance.

NOTE

The hop-waltz may also be done turning.

46. *Hopp Mor Annika*
(Swedish)

Record:
Victor-21618

BASIC STEPS

Step-hop; skip; polka.

FORMATION

Double circle is formed, partners facing; girl on the outside.

Dance

Introduction: Bow to the partner, join inside hands and face in the line of direction.

Measures

1-4	Take four step-hops forward.
1-4	Take four step-hops backward.
5-8	Take eight skips forward.
5-8	Take eight skips backward. Finish, facing

partner.

9 Stamp your right foot forward and, at the same time, clap partner's right hand. Bring the right foot back and clap your own hands.

10 Stamp your left foot forward and, at the same time, clap partner's left hand. Bring the left foot back and clap your own hands.

11 Clap partner's hands twice.

12 Clap your own hands twice.

9-12 Repeat.

13-20 Face in the line of direction and take eight polka steps forward.

Variation

13-20 Face your partner and join both hands, take eight slides clockwise, then eight slides counterclockwise.

47. *Irish Jig*
(Irish)

Record:
Victor-21616
(Irish Washerwoman)

BASIC STEPS

Skip; slide; hop; heel and toe.

FORMATION

Dancers form groups of six or eight in parallel lines, partners facing each other, hands joined.

DANCE

Part 1

Measures

1-4   Take four skips forward, four skips back.

5-8   Repeat 1-4.

9-10   Hands on the hips, hop on the right foot and tap the left toe to the side. Repeat the hop and tap on the same foot three times. Make a sound with the toe as it touches the floor.

11-12   Take four slides to the left, starting with the left foot.

13-16   Same as 9-12, but hop on the left foot, tap right and slide right.

Part 2

1-8   Repeat measures 1-8 of Part 1.

9-10   Hands on the hips, hop on the right foot and touch the left heel to the side. Repeat the hop and the heel touch on each foot three times. Make a sound with the heel as it touches the floor.

11-12   Take four slides to the right.

13-16   Repeat 9-12 in the opposite direction.

Part 3

1-8   Repeat the measures 1-8 of Part 1.

9-10   Hands on the hips, hop on the right foot and touch the left toe to the side; turn the toe in and the heel out. Hop on the right foot and touch the left heel to the side; turn the toe up. Repeat all again.

11-12   Take four slides right.

13-16   Repeat 9-12 in the opposite direction.

Repeat all.

48. *Little Brown Jug*

(American)

Record:

Folkraft G5003

BASIC STEPS

Slide; skip.

FORMATION

Double circle is formed, partners facing; the hands are joined and raised at shoulder height. The girl is on the outside.

DANCE

Counts

8   Girls touch the right heel to the side and then touch the right toe beside the left foot. They repeat heel and toe touching again and follow with four slides to the right. Boys do the same, starting with the opposite foot.

8   Repeat, touching the left heel and toe to the side. Take four slides left, returning to your place.

4   Clap hands to thighs three times; then clap your own hands three times.

4 Partners clap their right hands together three times and then clap their left hands together three times.

8 Hook right elbows with your partner and turn in circle twice with eight skips.

8 Repeat clapping.

8 Repeat turn, hooking the left elbows.

49. *Modern Virginia Reel*
(American)

Records:
Decca-2564A
Victor-20447

Basic Steps

Skip; slide; do-si-do; reel.

Formation

Sets of six or eight couples stand in parallel lines, partners facing.

Dance

Part 1

All couples perform the movements at the same time rather than the head and foot couples as in the original version. The basic step in this part is the skip.

Measures

1-4   Take four skips forward and four skips back.

5-8   Repeat 1-4.

9-12   Partners join right hands, turn once around, and return to place.

13-16   Repeat with the left hands joined.

1-4   Partners turn with both hands joined.

5-8   Do-si-do with partner.

9-16   Head couple joins hands and slides eight steps down the center of the set, and returns to place with eight slides.

Part 2

32   Reel, head couple starting. (See Glossary.)

Part 3

8   MARCH-All couples face toward the head of the set. The head couple leading, the girls march to the right and the boys to the left. When the head couple reaches the foot of the set, it makes an arch and all others pass under. The head couple is now at the foot of the set and the dance is repeated with a new head couple.

NOTE

If you are using the Decca record, have eight couples in a set.

50. *Oh Susanna Circle*
(American)

Record:
Folkraft F1017

Basic Steps
Slide; skip; do-si-do.

Formation
Partners stand in single circle, facing center, all hands joined. The girl is on the right of the boy.

Dance

Counts

16	Take eight slides to the right and eight to the left.
8	Take four skips to center and four skips back.
8	Repeat the skips to center and to the back.
8	Do-si-do with partner.
8	Do-si-do with neighbor.
8	Partners face, join hands at shoulder height, and take four slides to the center and four slides back.
8	Repeat sliding to center and back.
16	Promenade with partner.

VARIATION

A grand right and left may be substituted for promenade. At the end of the grand right and left, each person will have a new partner. Repeat the dance with the new partner.

51. *Pin Wheel Polka*

BASIC STEP

Polka.

FORMATION

Sets of two couples, partners facing, are arranged informally around the room.

DANCE

Measures

1-8   Couples in each set join hands and take seven polka steps to the left and three stamps in place.

1-8   They repeat 1-8, moving to the right. All drop hands on stamps and turn so that their right side is toward the center of the circle.

9-16   Join your right hand with the opposite partner. The arms will now be crossed to form a pin wheel. Keep the arms straight and pull away from the center. Take seven polka steps in the line of direction. Follow with three stamps. Turn on the three stamps to face in the opposite direction. Join left hands.

9-16   Repeat 9-16 in the new direction, but face center on three stamps.

Repeat all.

52. *Pop Goes the Weasel (Square)*
(American)

Record:
Victor-20151

BASIC STEPS

Skip; allemande; grand right and left; promenade.

FORMATION

Squares of eight are formed.

DANCE

Measures

1-6   The head couple leads out to the right and circles four hands around with the second couple.

7-8   The first couple "pops" under the arms of the second couple and leads on to the third couple.

9-16   Repeat with the third couple.

1-8   Repeat with the fourth couple.

9-13   Allemande left on the corner.

14-16   Swing partner.

Repeat all of the above measures, with the second couple leading out to the right. Do the same with the third and fourth couples.

After all figures have been completed, do a grand right and left all the way around then promenade.

53. *Ribbon Dance*
(English)

Record:
Victor-21619

BASIC STEPS

Walk; skip; polka.

FORMATION

Six couples are in two parallel lines, partners facing. Couples are numbered from one to six starting at the head of the set. The members of each couple hold a ribbon between them, two colors of crepe paper may be used, odd couples holding one color and even couples another. Odd numbered couples raise the ribbon high; even couples hold it low.

DANCE

Part 1

Use weaving step or over and under.

Measures

1-2   Couples 1 and 2 turn and face each other, 3 and 4 do the same, also 5 and 6. With four walking steps forward, couples 1 and 2 change places, couple 2 passing under the arch of couple 1. At the same time, couples 3 and 4 as well as 5 and 6 do the same, each even-numbered couple going under the arch.

3-4   All couples change back to place with four walking steps; the even couples hold the ribbons high this time and the odd couples go under the arch.

5-8   Repeat counts 1-4.

Part 2

9-12   All turn and face the head of the set, the girls dropping the ribbons. The head couple leads off with a skip, each partner turning to the outside of his line. Girls follow the girls and boys follow the boys.

13-16   When partners meet at the foot of the set, the girls take the ribbons again and they skip back to place holding the ribbons high.

Part 3

9-16   The head couple joins inside hands and takes polka steps down the center of the set under the arches made by the ribbons. The head couple remains at the foot of the set and the dance is repeated with the new head couple.

54. *Seven Jumps*
(Danish)

Record:
Victor-21617

BASIC STEP

Slide.

FORMATION

Single circle is formed, with hands joined.

DANCE

Part 1

Mcasures

1-8   Take eight slides to the right.

9-16   Take eight slides to the left.

17-18   Drop the hands, bend the right knee up, lower the leg slowly and hold.

Part 2

1-16   Repeat.

17-18   Bend the right knee up and then lower the leg.

17-18   Bend the left knee up and then lower the leg.

Part 3

1-16   Repeat.

17-18   Bend the right knee, lower the leg.

17-18   Bend the left knee, lower the leg.

17-18   Kneel on the right-knee leg.

Other parts of the dance are the same, but keep adding a new movement each time measures 17 and 18 are repeated, as follows:

Part 4. Kneel on the left knee.

Part 5. Place the right elbow on the floor.

Part 6. Place the left elbow on the floor.

Part 7. Place the head on the floor.

Repeat measures 1-16 to end the dance.

55. *Swing the Corner Lady (Square)*

Basic Steps

Allemande; do-si-do; promenade.

Formation

Squares of eight are formed.

DANCE

Measures

1-4   All join hands and take four steps forward and four back to place.

1-4   Repeat.

5-8   Allemande right with partner.

9-12   Allemande left with corner.

1-4   Do-si-do with partner.

1-4   Swing your corner lady.

5-12   Promenade with the corner lady.

Each lady now has a new partner. Repeat the dance until all are back to their original partners.

56. *Tantoli*
(Swedish)

Record:
Victor-20992

Basic Steps

Heel-toe polka; step-hop; hop-waltz.

Formation

Double circle is formed, facing in the line of direction, left side turned toward the center of the circle. Inside hands are joined.

Dance

Measures

1-4   Starting with the outside foot, take two heel-toe polka steps.

1-4   Repeat two heel-toe polka steps.

5-6   Hook right elbows with the partner and take four step-hops in circle to the right.

7-8   Repeat 5-6, hooking left elbows and turning left.

5-8   Face your partner, join hands and extend the arms to the side, shoulder high. Take eight hop-waltz steps in place. Repeat all.

57. *Tretur* (*Three Dance*)
(Danish)

Basic Steps

Run; step-hop; slide.

Formation

Squares of eight are formed.

Dance

Part 1

Measures

1-8   All join hands and do eight slides in a circle to the right, then repeat eight slides to the left.

1-8   Repeat the above.

Part 2

9-12   Couples one and three run forward with eight running steps. Couple three separates, allowing couple one to pass between.

13-16   The couples turn around and run eight steps back to place; couple one separates, allowing couple three to pass between.

9-16   Side couples two and four repeat the same.

Part 3

17-18   Couple one and three move toward each other with two step-hops.

19-22   Each boy hooks his right elbows with the opposite girl and turns once around with four step-hops.

23-24   Couple one and three take two step-hops backward to place.

17-24   Side couples repeat.

58. Two Head Ladies Cross Over
(American)

BASIC STEPS

Slide; promenade.

FORMATION

Squares of eight are formed.

DANCE

Part 1

Measures

1-4   Honor your partner and honor your corner.

5-12   All join hands and take eight slides right. Return to place with eight slides.

13-16   Swing your partner.

17-24   Promenade once around.

Part 2

1-4   The two head ladies cross over and stand by the opposite gentleman.

5-9   The two side ladies cross over and stand by the opposite gentleman.

10-12   Honor your corner, and honor your partner.

13-16   Swing the corner lady.

17-24   Promenade with the corner lady.

Part 3

1-16   All of part two is repeated, with the gentlemen changing places instead of the ladies.

13-24   Swing the corner lady and promenade with her.

Repeat parts 2 and 3 until all promenade with the original partners.

59. *Yankee Doodle*
(American)

Record:
Victor 20166

Yankee doodle went to town
Ridin' on a pony
He stuck a feather in his cap
And called it macaroni.

Chorus

Yankee doodle doodle do,
Yankee doodle dandy.
Mind the music and the step,
And with the girls be handy.

BASIC STEPS

Skip; gallop; polka.

FORMATION

Dancers form double circle, facing the line of direction, left side toward the center.

DANCE

Measures

1-8   Starting with the outside foot, take sixteen walking steps forward, raising knees high.

9-12   Chorus: Hook right elbows with your partner and take eight skips, circling around to place.

13-16   Repeat 9-12, hooking left elbows.

1-8   Take sixteen skip steps forward.

9-16   Repeat the chorus.

1-8   Take four gallop steps, starting with the right foot, then four gallop steps, starting with the left foot. Repeat right, then left.

9-16   Repeat the chorus.

1-8   Take eight polka steps forward.

9-16   Repeat the chorus.

SELF-TESTING ACTIVITIES

60. *Ankle Jump*

Stand with the feet together, bend your knees a little and grasp the ankles with your hands. In this position, jump over a chalk mark placed about one foot in front of the toes. The distance may be increased or lessened according to the ability of the group.

61. *Back Rocker and Get-Up*

Lie on the back and bend the knees. Reach forward and grasp the ankles firmly with your hands. Rock back and forth in this position several times in order to gain enough momentum to come to a standing position.

62. *Backward Roll*

Take a squat position with the weight on the balls of the feet. Place your fingers on the mat in front, tuck the head and round the back. With a push from the fingers and toes, roll backwards, keeping the body round like a ball throughout. Use the hands to help complete the roll by placing them on the mat by the shoulders and pushing when the weight passes over the shoulders. Keep the head tucked close to the body at all times and do not flatten your back or straighten out the legs.

The backward roll may be started from a standing position, dropping quickly to a squat position and rolling backward. Keep the body well rounded as before; always use a mat and give assistance.

63. *Bear Dance*

Take squat position and fold your arms across the chest. Extend the right leg forward, change bringing the right leg back and extending the left leg forward. Alternate in rapid succession. You may extend your legs to the side alternately instead of in front. You may also vary the position of the arms. You may place them on the hips or extend them straight to the side.

64. *Coffee Grinder*

Take a deep knee bend and place your left hand on the floor by your left side, keeping the elbow stiff. Extend both legs to the right so that the left side of the body is toward the floor. In this position, using the left arm as pivot, walk around in circle. Repeat, using the other arm as the pivot.

65. *Fish Hawk Dive*

Kneel on one knee, extend the other leg back, and stretch your arms to the side for balance. Bend forward and touch the floor with the head. Return to the starting position without losing balance. When this has been accomplished, try doing it without touching the floor with the extended leg. Do not touch the floor with either hand.

66. *Forward and Backward Roll Combination*

Do one forward roll and come to a standing position. Turn around immediately and do a backward roll. You may also do a forward roll with crossed legs and then uncross the legs on the turn. Use a mat.

67. *Forward Roll*

Take a deep knee bend and place your hands on the mat in front of your feet. Bend your head, tuck your chin close to the chest, and round the back. Then push from the toes and roll forward, momentarily shifting your weight on the hands. When the roll is completed, come to a standing position. It is important to keep the head tucked throughout and the body rounded like a ball. Always use a mat for this stunt and give assistance.

68. *Forward Roll, Grasping the Toes*

Before starting the roll, **take a squat** position and grasp the toes with your hands. In this position, tuck the head between the knees and roll forward. Try to maintain the grasp to the finish.

69. *Forward Roll with Crossed Legs*

Start in the same manner as a regular forward roll. Just before the finish, cross your feet and come to standing position with the feet still crossed. Use a mat.

70. *Full Squat*

Stand with the feet together. Place your hands behind the back and clasp the right wrist with the left hand. Bend the knees, keeping your feet flat on the floor and touch the floor with the fingers of the right hand. Without losing balance, return to standing position. Your heels must remain in contact with the floor at all times.

71. *Grapevine*

Stand with the feet together. Bend your knees and place the arms between your knees around in back of the ankles. Hold balance in this position thirty seconds or thirty counts. Run a contest to see who can maintain the position the longest.

72. *Heel Touch*

Jump in the air and raise both heels as high as possible behind you. Touch the heels with both hands.

73. *Human Ball*

Sit on the floor and bend your knees to the chest. Place your hands between the legs and around the outside of the ankles, and clasp hands in front of the ankles securely. In this position, rock to the left and right several times and then roll to right, falling on that side; roll over on the back, then to the left side and come to sitting position again. This should be a continuous motion once it gets started and is repeated several times.

74. *Kangaroo Leap*

Take a squat position and place the right hand on the floor by the right side. With a jump, extend your legs to the left side, keeping the body straight. Return to squat position and repeat this on the other side. Alternate several times.

75. *Knee Dip*

Take your weight on the left foot, bend your right knee and grasp it with the right hand. Extend the left arm to the side for balance. Bend the supporting leg, touch the floor with the right knee, and return to standing position. Repeat this with the opposite leg. Use a mat.

76. *Knee Jump*

Kneel on both knees and swing the arms backward. With a strong pull, swing the arms forward and upward and jump to the feet.

77. *Leg Twirl*

Stand with your weight on the right foot and grasp the toe of the left foot with the left hand, extending the left leg forward. Make a complete turn, hopping on the right foot. Then try to make two or three turns in succession.

78. *Rocking Chair*

Two children sit on the floor, facing each other, with their knees bent and their feet flat on the floor. Each sits on the other's feet and clasps the other's hands firmly. In this position, they rock back and forth. The first child rocks back and pulls the second child up. The first child should keep his feet in contact with the second child. Then the second child sits down, rolls back and pulls the first child up. This is repeated several times. It is suggested that two children of nearly the same size work together.

79. *Twister*

Partners stand facing each other. The first child joins his right hand with the second child's left hand. The first child steps over the joined hands with his left foot and the second child does the same with his right foot. They are now back to back. The first child brings the right foot over his joined arms and the second child lifts his left foot over his joined arms. Then the partners are back to the starting position, facing each other. Repeat several times without stopping.

80. *Walrus Walk*

Take a squat position and place your hands on the floor between your legs. Extend the legs backward. Walk forward on the hands and drag the feet. Keep your back straight. Travel to a given distance.

81. *Wheelbarrow*

The first child takes a squat position, places his hands on the floor, and extends the legs backward. The second child stands behind the first one, grasps his ankles and raises them about waist high. In this position, they walk forward a designated distance. This may be used as a race with couples competing against each other.

82. *Wicket Jump*

Take a squat position on the floor and place both hands on the floor in front of your legs. Extend the legs backward so that the weight now falls on the hands and toes; keep your back straight. Bend the hips and tuck the knees up to the chest. Then slide the feet between the arms without removing the hands from the floor. The arms represent the wicket. Next, try to jump between the arms without touching the floor with your feet.

Grade Five

There may be a rapid increase in weight for girls while boys tend to lag in rate of growth. There is a great interest in acquiring physical skills. Considerable time and energy are spent in perfecting these skills as group approval is often determined by ability to perform. Boys and girls enjoy participation in team play, but the boys are more active and rougher than the girls.

This age group shows the ability to budget time to greater advantage and seem to do less aimless rushing around than children in the lower grades. Individual differences, although apparent before, tend to become more pronounced. Individual abilities are more noticeable and encouragement should be given to improve these aptitudes.

There is more interest in organized and competitive games and children are able to follow set rules and abide by group decisions. Clubs also are important at this age. Children show great loyalty to their own groups or organizations and enjoy keeping secrets with other members. Boys and girls prefer to play separately. There is little feeling of companionship between them.

SUGGESTED LESSON PLANS

September

Activities	Equipment	Section
GAMES		
Soccer Skills	Several balls	25
Army-Navy Ball	One ball	1
Soccer Tag	One ball	26
Last Couple Run		21
RELAYS		
Soccer Dribble Relay	One ball for each team	43
Partner Dribble and Pass Relay	One ball for each team	39
DANCES		
Ace of Diamonds	Victor Record 20989	46
Sicilian Circle	Victor Record 20639	62
	Victor Record 22991	
	Woodhull Record 36403	
SELF-TESTING ACTIVITIES		
Ankle Toss	A small ball or bean bag	66
Toe Kick		81

October

Activities	Equipment	Section
GAMES		
Triplet Tag		28
Corner Kick Soccer	One ball	11
Cowboy Round-Up		13
Indian-Club Chase	Six Indian clubs or other objects	19
DANCES		
Donegal Country Dance		49
Polka Couple Dance	Any polka record	57
SELF-TESTING ACTIVITIES		
Novelty Walk		75
Heel Jump		68

November

Activities	Equipment	Section
GAMES		
Long Base	One ball, one Indian club	22
Hit the Target	One ball for each team	18
RELAYS		
Run and Pass Back Relay	One ball for each team	41
Bounce Ball Relay	One ball for each team	30
DANCES		
Csebogár	Victor Record 20992	48
Hinky-Dinky, Parlee Voo	Folkraft Record 1059	54
SELF-TESTING ACTIVITIES		
Wall Push		82
Midget Walk		72

December

Activities	Equipment	Section
GAMES		
Basketball Skills	Several balls	5
Three-Court Dodge Ball	One ball	27
Keep Away	One ball	20
RELAYS		
Circle Race Relay	One ball for each team	32
Heel-Grasp Relay		36
DANCES		
Finnish Reel		50
Skater's Scottische		63
SELF-TESTING ACTIVITIES		
Human Arch		70
Single-Leg Squat		77

January

Activities	Equipment	Section
GAMES		
'Round the Clock	One ball for each team	24
End Ball	One ball	14
RELAYS		
Crooked Walk Relay		35
Indian Club Change Relay	Three Indian clubs or other objects for each team	37
DANCES		
The Hatter	Victor Record 20449	65
Turkey in the Straw	Victor Record 22131	64
SELF-TESTING ACTIVITIES		
Team Forward Rolls	A mat	80
Stick Pull		88
Rooster Fight		87

February

Activities	Equipment	Section
GAMES		
Basketball Pass Contest	One ball for each team	4
Catching Bounders	One ball	10
RELAYS		
Zig-Zag Run Relay	Four Indian clubs or other objects for each team	45
Race Track Relay	Four Indian clubs, four batons or other objects	40
Crab Walk Relay		34
DANCE		
Heel and Toe Polka	Ford Record 107A	52
Schottische Hop	Folkraft Record 117B	60
SELF-TESTING ACTIVITIES		
Monkey Roll	A mat	73
Hand Wrestle		86
Finger Pull		85

March

Activities	Equipment	Section
GAMES		
Captain's Base	One ball	8
Goal Keep Away	One ball, one basketball goal	16
RELAYS		
Leap Frog Relay		38
Back to Back Relay		29
Shuttle Run and Pass Relay	One ball for each team	42
DANCES		
Highland Schottische	Victor Record 21616	53
Sellenger's Round	Victor Record 20445B	61
SELF-TESTING ACTIVITIES		
Sitting Balance		78
Stick Wrestle		88
Bull Fight		83

April

Activities	Equipment	Section
GAMES		
Hit Pin Kick Ball	One rubber ball and four Indian clubs	17
Bowling	Three Indian clubs and a ball for each team	6
Catch the Golden Eagle	Seven Indian clubs or other objects	9
RELAY		
Wheelbarrow Race Relay		44
DANCES		
Glow Worm	Folkraft Record 11044	51
Irish Washerwoman	Victor Record 21616	55
SELF-TESTING ACTIVITIES		
Seal Slap		76
Chair Dip	A chair	67
Hop Contest	Pieces of chalk	69

May

Activities	Equipment	Section
GAMES		
Couple Tag		12
Brothers		7
RELAYS		
Chain Hop Relay		31
Club Ball Relay	One Indian club and one ball for each team	33
DANCES		
Kalvelis	Folkraft Record 1051A Folkraft Record M301	56
Rakes of Mallow	Folkraft Record 33505F	58
SELF-TESTING ACTIVITIES		
Mule Kick		74
Tandem		79

June

Activities	Equipment	Section
GAMES		
Ball Tag	One ball	2
Base Running Contest	Four bases and a stop watch or a watch with a second hand	3
Five Jumps		15
Newcomb	One ball and a net or a rope	23
DANCES		
American Quadrille	Victor Record 20447A Woodhull Record 36403	47
Sailor's Hornpipe	Victor Record 21685	59
SELF-TESTING ACTIVITIES		
Jump the Stick		71
Club Fight	An Indian club	84

GAMES

1. *Army Navy Ball*

Equipment: One ball.

FORMATION

Two equal teams, "Army" and "Navy" take their places in the playing area on two parallel lines opposite each other. The lines are about eight to ten feet apart.

ACTION

The ball is passed back and forth between the two teams. When a signal is given, the passing is stopped and the team not in possession of the ball scatters about the playing area. The player with the ball attempts to hit one of the members of the opposing team. If he succeeds, he scores a point for his team and the game is resumed. If he fails, the ball is passed to another player on his team who attempts to hit someone. After a team has had two chances and no one has been hit, the game is started again. The team with the larger number of points, at the end of the playing time, wins.

NOTE

See that each team has an equal opportunity to put players out. Do not just alternate sides.

2. Ball Tag

Equipment: One ball.

FORMATION

Players are scattered about the playing area. One player is "It" and has a ball.

ACTION

"It" attempts to tag a runner with the ball or hit him with the ball below the waist. Any player touched by the ball becomes "It" and the game continues. If "It" throws the ball and does not hit anyone, he must recover the ball.

3. Base Running Contest

Equipment: Four bases and a stop watch or a watch with a second hand.

FORMATION

The playing area is a softball diamond and all players are behind the home plate.

ACTION

One player stands on the home plate and, on signal, runs around the bases touching each one in order, finishing at the home plate. Failure to touch a base disqualifies a player. The players run, one at a time, while the instructor times and records each one's time as he crosses the home plate. The player with the lowest time wins.

4. *Basketball Pass Contest*

Equipment : One ball for each team.

FORMATION

Divide the group into equal teams of eight or ten players. Each team forms a single circle, facing center.

ACTION

One player in each circle has a ball which he passes at a given signal to any other player in the circle, preferably to a player opposite. The players continue to pass the ball back and forth across the circle to any member of the team. The object of the game is to make as many completed passes as possible in a given length of time. The circle making the greatest number of completed passes wins. One player is appointed to count the passes. Any passes dropped should not be counted.

Before the game starts, designate the type of pass, such as chest pass, underhand pass, etc., to be used. Allow about two minutes playing time before the signal is given to stop. Start the game again, using another type of pass. Accuracy and speed are important.

5. *Basketball Skills*

STANCE FOR PASSES

Stand with the feet in a forward-backward stride position and most of the weight on the back foot. As the ball is released, transfer the weight to the forward foot.

PASSING THE BALL

1. Short passes are usually better and safer.
2. Pass the ball ahead of your teammate.
3. Control the speed of your pass. Hard passes are difficult to handle.
4. Use a variety of passes.
5. Step in the direction of your pass and follow through with the arms, elbows in.
6. Try to pass the ball to the best possible position for your teammate to catch it.

CATCHING THE BALL

1. Keep your eyes on the ball.
2. Cup your hands, fingers relaxed and turned out.
3. Bend the elbows and knees slightly as the ball comes toward you. This is called "giving" with the ball.
4. Try to get yourself in the best possible position to receive the pass and go to meet it. Don't wait for the pass to come to you.
5. When catching the ball below the waist, point the fingers down. If the ball is received at the waist hold the fingers straight ahead, above the waist, point the fingers up.

TYPES OF PASSES

Chest. Hold the ball in both hands in front of the chest. Spread the fingers well and do not touch the ball with the heel of the hand. Release the ball by extending the arms forward and snap the wrists. Keep your elbows close to the body.

Bounce. Hold the ball with both hands and, just before it is released, one hand should leave the ball as the other pushes it toward the floor. Pass the ball so that it bounces three feet in front of the receiver, waist high.

Two-Hand Underhand. Hold the ball waist high or a little below. The pass may be made on either side or in front of the body. To release the ball, swing the arms forward and upward.

One-Hand Underhand. Hold the ball in the palm of the right hand, below the hip, on the right side of the body. Swing the right arm forward to release the ball. Do the reverse when passing with the left hand.

Two-Hand Overhead Pass. Hold the ball over the head with the elbows slightly bent. Release the ball with a snap of the wrist and fingers.

6. *Bowling*

Equipment : Three Indian clubs and one ball for each team.

FORMATION

The three Indian clubs are placed four or five inches apart to form a triangle with the apex toward the players. There is one set of Indian clubs for each team. The teams are in single file formation behind a line, about twenty feet from the clubs. There is a "Scorer" and a "Pin Boy" for each team.

ACTION

The first player in each line rolls the ball, attempting to knock all three pins down at once. If he succeeds, it is called a "Strike" and he receives five points for his team. If he knocks down two clubs, he gets three points, and one point for one club. The Pin

Boy sets up the clubs and the Scorer records the points. Continue until all have had a turn. The team with the higher score wins. Play the game again, using different players for Scorers and Pin Boys. If the group is small, the game may be played on an individual basis.

7. Brothers

FORMATION

Partners are in a double circle. The inside circle faces clockwise and the outer circle, counterclockwise.

ACTION

At a given signal, each circle marches around the room in the direction which it is facing. Another signal is given and the players run to find their partners (Brothers), turn back to back, hook elbows, and sit down. The last couple to sit down is eliminated from the game. The circle reforms and the game is restarted. The game continues until all but one couple are eliminated. If the group is large, the last two or three couples may be eliminated each time.

VARIATIONS

Use other stunts in place of back to back, such as:

1. Horse and rider: one player kneels and places his hands on the floor and the other straddles his back.

2. Wheelbarrow position: the first player takes a squat position, places his hands on the floor, and extends the legs backward. The second player stands behind the first one, grasps his ankles and raises them about waist high.

8. *Captain's Base*

Equipment: One ball.

FORMATION

There are two equal teams, "Red" and "Blue." Each team has a "Captain" and a "Guard." Two circles are drawn on the floor, one inside the other. The players of the two teams stand in alternate positions in each circle. Each team's Captain and Guard stand in the center of the inner circle. The Captains stand on a base marked out on the floor.

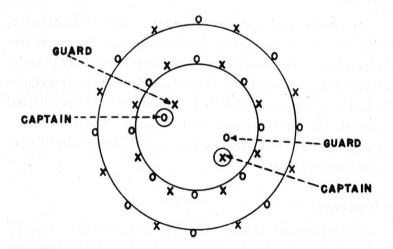

ACTION

One of the players in the outer circle has a ball and, at a signal to start, he attempts to pass the ball to the Captain of his team. The other team tries to intercept the ball. If they are successful, they try to pass the ball to their Captain. The Guards may move about in the center area, but the Captains must remain on base. A point is made each time the Captain of a team succeeds in catching the ball. After each point, the players of the inside circle and the outside circle exchange places and new Guards and Captains are chosen. The team with the higher score, at the end of the playing time, wins.

9. *Catch the Golden Eagle*

Equipment: Seven Indian clubs or other objects.

FORMATION

Two teams of equal number stand on opposite sides of the playing area in single lines behind a starting line. Seven Indian clubs are placed several yards apart. A circle is drawn around the club in the center which represents the "Golden Eagle."

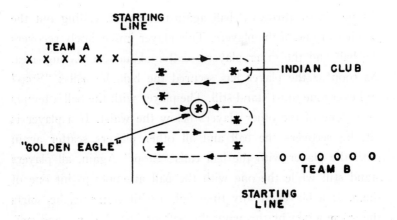

ACTION

A signal is given and the first player in each team runs forward around the Indian clubs, following the path indicated. Each tries to grab the Golden Eagle. The player who succeeds, scores a point for his team. If there is a tie, both grabbing the center club at the same time, no point is scored. The next player in each line repeats the action and the game continues until all have had a turn. The team with the higher score wins.

10. *Catching Bounders*

Equipment: One ball.

FORMATION

A rectangular playing area is marked out near a wall. The players are numbered and stand behind a line, about fifteen feet from the wall.

ACTION

One player throws a ball against the wall, calling out the number of one of the players. This player immediately recovers the ball and the other players scatter about the playing area. As soon as the player has secured the ball, he calls: "Stop" and everyone must stand still. The player with the ball attempts to hit one of the other players below the waist. If a player is hit, he recovers the ball and all other players scatter again until the player with the ball calls "Stop." Again, all players stand still while the one with the ball attempts to hit one of them. If a player at any time fails to hit someone, he starts the game again by throwing the ball against the wall and calling the number of one of the players. The play proceeds as before. The players must stay within the designated playing area except to recover the ball when it goes out of bounds.

11. *Corner Kick Soccer*

Equipment: One ball.

FORMATION

There are two equal teams, "A" and "B," which take places at opposite ends of a rectangular playing area behind a goal line. One player from each corner goes to the center of the field. These players are called "Forwards." The other players behind the goal lines are "Guards." A ball is placed in the center of the field.

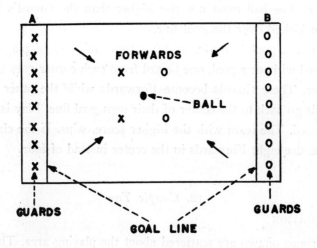

ACTION

The ball is given to the Forward of team "A" who attempts to dribble the ball and kick it over the opponent's goal thus scoring a point for his team. The Forwards of team "B" try to seize the ball and kick it over their opponents' goal line.

Forwards may move around freely in the playing area between the two goal lines. The Guards must remain behind their goal line and try to prevent the ball from passing over the goal line by kicking it away from the goal and out into the field of play. They cannot use their hands to stop the ball.

General rules:

a. If a player touches the ball with his hands, pushes, or uses unnecessary roughness the ball is awarded to the opposing team.

b. If the ball goes out of bounds, it is kicked in by a player of the opposing team.

c. The ball must not rise higher than the Guard's waist when kicked over the goal line.

After a goal is made, or after three minutes of play have elapsed without a goal, one Guard from each corner goes to the center. These Guards become Forwards while the other Forwards go back to the center of their own goal line. Play is then resumed. The team with the higher score, wins. If the class is large, use eight Forwards in the center instead of four.

12. *Couple Tag*

FORMATION

Groups of two are scattered about the playing area. The inside hands of each couple are joined. One player is "It."

ACTION

"It" tries to grasp the free hand of one member of a couple and if he succeeds the other member becomes "It" and the game continues.

13. *Cowboy Round-Up*

FORMATION

Players are scattered around the playing area. Five players, selected to be "Cowboys," join hands in a line. The other players are called "Steers."

ACTION

The Cowboys attempt to capture one or more of the Steers by encircling them. Any Steers captured are eliminated. This continues until all but five of the Steers have been captured. The five remaining become Cowboys and the game is started again.

14. *End Ball*

Equipment : One ball.

FORMATION

The group is divided into two equal teams. Four players from each team are "Basemen" who take their places in the end zones, at opposite ends of a rectangular playing space. The

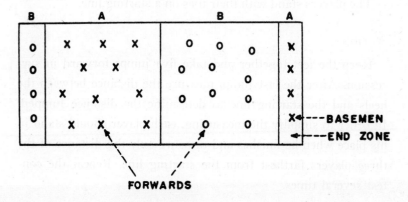

FORWARDS

other members are "Forwards" who stand in their respective courts on each side of the center line.

ACTION

The ball is put in play at the center line by tossing it between two Forwards of opposing teams. Each tries to tap the ball to a member of his own team. The team obtaining the ball, attempts to throw it to one of its own Basemen in the end zone. Each time one of the Basemen succeeds in catching the ball, one point is scored for that team. The ball is put back into play again at the center after each point. The team having the higher score, at the end of the playing time, wins. The ball is awarded the opposing team out of bounds for any of the following fouls or violations:

1. Pushing, holding, or tripping.
2. Walking with the ball.
3. Stepping over the center line.
4. Holding the ball more than five seconds.

15. *Five Jumps*

FORMATION

The players stand with their toes on a starting line.

ACTION

Keep the feet together and take five jumps forward in succession. After the last jump, measure the distance between the heels and the starting line to determine the distance jumped. In order to simplify the measuring, each player should stand in his place when he finishes and measure only the distance of the three players farthest from the starting line. Repeat the contest several times.

16. *Goal Keep Away*

The game is played in the same manner as "Keep Away," *
except that when a team makes five completed passes in succession, a free throw for goal from any spot under the basketball goal is awarded a member of that team. A point is scored
if the goal is made. If the goal is made or missed, the ball is
put back in play again from a point on the side line by a player
from the opposing team. Only one basketball goal is needed for
this game.

17. *Hit Pin Kick Ball*

Equipment: One rubber ball and four Indian clubs.

FORMATION

A softball diamond is used but the bases are marked with
chalk and one Indian club is placed on each base. There are two
equal teams. One takes its place in the field and the other is
up at bat. Each team consists of a catcher, pitcher, first, second,
and third basemen, one or two shortstops, and three fielders
(right, left, and center).

ACTION

The game is played like kick ball † except that to put a player
out after he has kicked the ball, the Indian club on the base
must be knocked down with the ball before the runner reaches
the base. This is done by throwing the ball at the Indian club.

* See section 20 for rules of "Keep Away."
† See grade four, section 16 for kick ball.

When the kicker is kicking the ball, he must stand a little to one side of the home plate to avoid knocking over the Indian club.

VARIATION

The ball may be batted as in softball, but use a rubber ball instead of a softball.

18. *Hit the Target*

Equipment : One ball for each team. Targets (circles) are drawn on a wall, three feet from the floor and three feet in diameter.

FORMATION

Teams are in single lines behind a pass line which is fourteen feet from the wall and parallel to it.

ACTION

The first player in each line has a ball which he throws at the target. He is allowed five chances to hit the target and scores one point each time the ball hits the wall within the circle. Each player has a turn. The team having the highest score wins. Any style of pass may be used, but an underhand pass is suggested as most effective. If a player steps over the line when throwing the ball, the pass does not count. When the group is small, the game may be played on an individual, rather than a team, basis.

VARIATION

Shorten the throwing distance to ten or twelve feet and see how many times a player can hit the target in one minute. The ball is caught on the bounce. The game may be played on an individual or team basis.

19. *Indian-Club Chase*

Equipment: Six Indian clubs or other objects.

FORMATION

Place the Indian clubs in a row, about three feet apart, at one end of the playing area. Establish a starting line parallel to the clubs at the opposite end of the area. Divide the players into groups of seven. They take their places in lines across the area behind the starting line.

INDIAN CLUBS

♣ ♣ ♣ ♣ ♣ ♣

STARTING LINE

LINE A	X X X X X X X
LINE B	X X X X X X X
LINE C	X X X X X X X

ACTION

At a starting signal, all players in line "A" run forward each trying to obtain a club. The player unable to obtain a club is eliminated. The clubs are replaced and the players in line "B" do the same. Continue until all lines have run once.

Now remove one club and repeat the game with six players in each line. The play continues until there is only one player left in each line.

20. *Keep Away*

Equipment: One ball.

FORMATION

Two teams with an equal number of players are scattered about a rectangular playing area. It is suggested that one team is marked in some manner so that the players are easily distinguished.

ACTION

The object of the game is for one team to make five consecutive passes. If successful, that team scores one point. The ball is put into play by a player from one team who stands outside the playing area. He passes it to one of his teammates who calls: "One" if he catches it. The one who caught the ball then passes it to another player on his team who calls: "Two." This continues until five passes have been made or the ball is intercepted by the opposing team. If the opposing team intercepts the ball, this team starts counting passes, attempting also to make five in a row.

General rules

1. If a player pushes or uses unnecessary roughness, the player fouled is allowed an unguarded pass and any previous passes made count.

2. If a player walks with the ball, a player from the opposing team is given the ball to throw it in from outside the playing area.

3. If the ball goes out of bounds, it is put back into play by an opponent on the side line nearest the point it went out of bounds.

4. If two people catch the ball at the same time, the ball is tossed between two players of the opposing teams while any earned passes are cancelled. After a point is made, a player from the opposing team throws the ball in from the side line and the game continues. The team having the greater number of points, at the end of the playing time, wins.

21. *Last Couple Run*

Equipment: One ball.

FORMATION

The class is divided into couples and they stand in a double line. One extra player is the "Catcher" and has a ball. He stands about twenty feet in front of the group with his back to them.

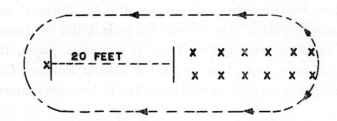

ACTION

To start the game, the Catcher calls: "Last couple run" and the last couple in the line runs toward the front. The right player on the right side of the double line, and the left player on the left side try to join hands in front of the Catcher before the catcher tags them with the ball or hits them with the ball below the waist. The Catcher cannot chase the runners or try to hit them before they are in line with him. He must not turn his head to see when the runners are coming. If the Catcher succeeds in tagging or hitting one of the players before they can clasp hands, the player tagged or hit becomes the Catcher. The first Catcher and the partner of the tagged player form a couple and take their places at the head of the line. If neither one of the last couple is caught, both take their places at the head of the line and the same player remains the Catcher, starting the play again. If the class is large, two or three groups may play the game at the same time.

22. *Long Base*

Equipment : One ball ; one Indian club.

FORMATION

There are two teams : one designated to be "Runners" and the other "Fielders." The Runners line up in double line formation behind a starting line. There is one extra player, the "Batter" who stands between the two lines of Runners. One neutral player may bat for each team. The Fielders are scattered

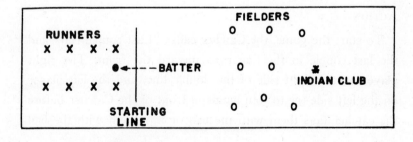

about the playing area. One Indian club is placed at the opposite
end of the playing area from the Runners.

ACTION

The Batter hits the ball off the palm of his left hand with
the clenched fist of his right into the playing area. As soon as
the ball has been hit, the first two runners run toward the Indian
club, go around it, and return to their places. Each player must
go around the club from the opposite direction.

The Fielders attempt to put the Runners out by hitting them
with the ball before they return to the starting line. The Fielders
are not allowed to walk with the ball, but they may pass it
around in order to be in a better position to hit or touch one
of the Runners with the ball.

A Runner tagged or hit by the ball is out and when a team
has three outs, it changes places with the Fielders. A run is
scored every time a player crosses the finish line without being
hit or tagged. The team having more runs, after an equal number of times at bat, wins.

23. *Newcomb*

Equipment: One ball and one volley ball net or badminton net.
A rope may be used in place of a net.

FORMATION

The net or rope is placed about seven feet from the ground
across the center of a rectangular playing area. Divide the group
into two teams, "A" and "B." Place one team on each side
of the net.

ACTION

To start the game, a player from team "A" is given the ball which he throws over the net. Any player from team "B" may attempt to catch the ball and return it across the net. Play continues back and forth until a team makes one of the following errors:

1. Fails to catch the ball.
2. Throws the ball out of bounds.
3. Holds the ball more than five seconds before throwing it.

One point is scored for the opposing team for any of the preceding offenses. The team with the higher score at the end of the playing time wins.

24. 'Round the Clock

Equipment: One ball for each team.

FORMATION

Divide the class into teams of six or eight players. Each team forms a circle, the players about eight feet apart. One player in each circle is "Captain." He has the ball and keeps the score.

ACTION

At a signal to start, each Captain passes the ball to the player on his left and each player, in turn, does the same around the circle. When the ball returns to the Captain, he calls out: "One" and continues to pass the ball. The Captain calls out the number of completed rounds each time he receives the ball. When twelve rounds have been completed, the Captain holds up the ball to indicate that his team is finished. The circle first completing twelve rounds wins. Repeat the game several times using a different type of pass each time. Some suggested passes are: chest, underhand, bounce, and overhead.

25. *Soccer Skills*

DRIBBLING

Dribbling is advancing the ball forward by a series of taps with the inside of the right and left foot alternately. Step left and tap the ball with the right foot near the toe, step right and tap the ball with the left foot. Keep the ball close to the feet at all times. In teaching the dribble, have the players tap the ball forward using only the right foot. Repeat using only the left. Then have them use both alternately.

PASSING

To pass the ball diagonally forward or sideward right, take the weight on the right foot and swing the left leg back and diagonally forward contacting the ball with the inside of the foot. Do the reverse for a pass to the left. In more advanced play, the player learns to use the outside of his foot too.

KICKING FORWARD

To make a long kick forward, place the weight on the left foot swinging the right leg backward, then forward to meet the ball with the toe pointing down so that the force that propels the ball comes from the instep. To avoid injury, never kick the ball with the end of the toes.

Stopping the Ball

Use the foot stop for a slow rolling ball. Place the weight on the left foot, raising the right foot about twenty inches from the ground. Flex the ankle so that the toe is up and the heel is down. As the ball comes toward you, bring the sole of the right foot down on top of the ball. This may be done with either foot.

26. *Soccer Tag*

Equipment: One rubber ball or one soccer ball.

Formation

Players are scattered about the playing area. The shape of the area is not important, but its limits must be clearly marked. One player who is "It" has a ball.

Action

"It" kicks the ball trying to hit another player with it. The ball should be kicked or tapped lightly and should not hit the player above his waist. A player hit by the ball is "It." The game continues. The ball should not be touched with the hands at any time. If the playing area is large, two balls may be used.

Variation

A player receives a point if he:
   1. Is touched with the ball.
   2. Touches the ball with his hands.

3. Runs out of the playing area to avoid being hit.

When a player accumulates three points he is eliminated from the game.

27. *Three-Court Dodge Ball*

Equipment : One ball.

FORMATION

The players are divided into three equal teams. Two lines are drawn across a rectangular playing area, dividing it into three equal courts. One team stands in each court.

ACTION

One player in the center court is given a ball and, at a signal to start, he attempts to hit one of the opposing players on either team. If he succeeds, the player hit is eliminated from the game. As soon as the ball hits the ground it may be recovered by any player. Each time a player is hit, he is eliminated. Players may move about freely in their own court, but cannot go outside except to recover the ball when it goes out of bounds.

After two minutes of play, the game is stopped and the

players eliminated from each team are counted. One point is scored against each team for every player eliminated. Play is resumed again with a different team in the center. All players eliminated may start again and the game continues as before. Rotate the teams so that each has a turn in the center. After three playing periods, total the numbers eliminated. The team with the lowest score wins.

28. *Triplet Tag*

FORMATION

Groups of three with hands joined are scattered about the play area. One group is "It" and carries a piece of red cloth to represent a flag.

ACTION

The "It" group tries to tag another group of three. Hands must be joined at all times. When a group is tagged, it is given the red flag and the game continues. Any group tagged more than twice is eliminated from the game.

RELAYS

29. *Back to Back Relay*

An even number of players are on each team in single lines behind a starting line. Each team pairs off in couples. The first couple in each line stands back to back and hooks elbows. In this position, they run forward to a turning line and back to place. The next couple does the same.

30. *Bounce Ball Relay*

Teams are in single lines behind a starting line which is thirty feet from a wall. A "Pass" line is drawn twelve feet from the wall and parallel to it. The first player in each line has a ball and runs forward to the Pass line throwing the ball against the wall and catching it on the bounce. The player must catch the ball on the first bounce. If he fails to do this, he must continue to throw the ball until he catches it correctly. If he steps over the line, he must also throw the ball again. As soon as the player catches the ball correctly, he runs back and gives it to the next player in line. The team finishing first wins.

31. *Chain Hop Relay*

An even number of players on each team are in single lines behind a starting line. Each team pairs off in couples. The first player steps in front of the second player and both stand on the left foot extending the right hand. The second player places his left hand on the shoulder of the first player. In this position, they hop forward to a turning line, exchange places, and hop back. The second couple should be ready to go as soon as the first returns. For variation, have four players form a chain instead of two.

32. *Circle Race Relays*

Equal teams form single circles. Players face the center, standing a few feet apart in the circle. Be sure that the circles are of equal size. One player in each circle has a ball. At a given signal, he runs around the outside of the circle and returns to place, passing the ball to the player on his right. This player repeats the process and the game continues until all have run. The last player holds the ball high when he completes his turn to indicate that his team has finished.

VARIATION

1. Bounce and catch the ball while running around the outside of the circle.

2. Dribble or bounce the ball without catching it while running around the circle.

33. *Club Ball Relay*

There are four teams. Teams "A" and "B" compete against each other, and "C" competes against "D." All teams are in single lines behind a starting line. An Indian club or other object is placed in front of each team at the opposite ends of the playing area. The first player in each line runs forward

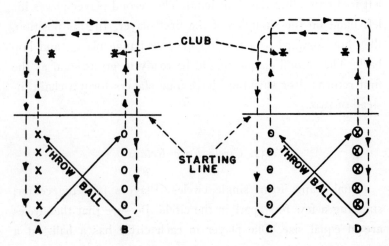

around both clubs and goes to the end of the opposing team instead of his own. When he gets there, he throws the ball to the second player on his team. This continues until all have run and all players are in the opposite team's line.

The game is repeated with the winners of "A" and "B" teams playing the winners of "C" and "D" and the losers playing the losers.

34. *Crab Walk Relay*

Teams are in single lines behind a starting line. The first player in each line squats down on the floor, places his weight on his hands and feet, and walks forward a designated distance in this position. Without turning around he returns to place, touching off the next player.

35. *Crooked Walk Relay*

Teams are in single lines behind a starting line. The first player in each line steps forward on his left foot and crosses his right foot behind his left going as far forward as possible before stepping on his right foot. Now he crosses his left foot behind his right and reaches as far forward as possible. He continues the step alternating right and left to a turning line. Then he runs back to place, touching off the next player.

36. *Heel Grasp Relay*

Teams are in single lines behind a starting line. The first player in each line bends his knees and grasps his heels with each hand moving forward to a turning line and back to place touching off the next player in line.

37. *Indian-Club Change Relay*

Teams are in single lines behind a starting line. Draw a circle on the floor a few feet in front of each team and place three Indian clubs, or any other object, in each circle. Draw a second circle twenty feet in front of the first circle. The first player in each team picks up one Indian club, runs forward, and places it in the second circle. He does the same with each club and when he has finished, he runs back and touches off the second player. The second player runs to the second circle in front of his line, returns each club separately to the first circle, and touches off the next player who repeats the procedure followed by the first player.

38. *Leap Frog Relay*

Teams are in single lines behind a starting line. A finish line is drawn parallel to the starting line at the opposite end of the playing area. The first player in each line runs forward a few feet and gets down on his hands and knees. The second player runs forward, leaps over the first player, and takes his position on hands and knees a few feet in front of him. This continues until all have run. Then the first player gets up, leaps over the backs of all the players, runs to the finish line, and stays there. The second player does the same and the game continues until all are behind the finish line. Be sure that the hands are well under the body so that they are not stepped on.

39. *Partner Dribble and Pass Relay*

There are an equal number of players on each team behind a starting line. Each team pairs off in couples. The first couple in each line has a ball which they move forward toward a turning line dribbling and passing the ball between them. At the turning line, the ball is stopped with the foot and the partners return to their original places in the same manner, passing the ball to the next couple in line. A team is disqualified if a player touches the ball with his hands.

40. *Race Track Relay*

There are four teams, each taking position at one corner of a rectangular playing area. An Indian club is placed about four feet in from each corner to form a track. The players must run between the club and the outside line. The first player in each

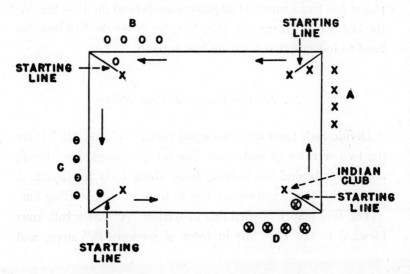

line has a baton or other object and steps up to the starting line. He runs forward around the track and returns to place handing the baton to the next player. This continues until all have run. The team finishing first wins.

VARIATION

Any runner who is able to tag another runner puts that player and his team out of the race. The game continues until only one team is left.

41. *Run and Pass Back Relay*

Teams are in single lines behind a starting line. A "Pass" line is marked off about twenty feet away, opposite the starting line. The first player in each line has a ball, runs forward to the Pass line, turns, and throws the ball back to the second player. The first player stays behind the Pass line. This continues until every player has had a turn and all players are behind the Pass line. As the last player crosses the Pass line, he raises the ball over his head to indicate that his team has finished.

42. *Shuttle Run and Pass Relay*

Divide each team into two equal parts, "A" and "B." Have the two sections of each team line up in a single line, facing each other behind the starting lines, about forty feet apart. A "Pass" line is marked off ten feet in front of each starting line.

The first player in each line in section "A" has a ball, runs forward to the Pass line in front of section "B," stops, and passes the ball to the first player on his team in section "B." After he has passed the ball, he goes to the end of the line in section "B." The player who receives the ball runs forward to the Pass line in front of section "A," stops, and passes the ball to the next player in section "A." This continues until all have had a turn and are in opposite lines.

VARIATION

Dribble or bounce the ball to the Pass line instead of carrying it.

43. *Soccer Dribble Relay*

The teams are in single lines behind a starting line. Mark off the turning points in front of each team at the opposite end of the area. The first player in each line has a ball which he dribbles forward using only the right foot, going around the turning point and returning to place. The second player does the same and the game continues until all have had a turn. Repeat the game, using only the left foot. When the game is repeated a third time use both feet.

44. *Wheelbarrow Race Relay*

An even number of players are on each team in single line formation behind a starting line. Each team pairs off in couples. The first couple of each team is on the starting line. One player places his hands on the floor and extends his legs out behind him while the other player stands behind and grasps the legs of his partner raising them waist high. In this position, they travel forward a designated distance. The players then exchange places and return to the starting line. The second couple should be ready to go as soon as the first returns.

45. *Zig-Zag Run Race Relay*

Teams are in single lines behind a starting line. Four Indian clubs, or other objects, are placed about four feet apart in front of each team. The first player in each line runs to the right of the first club and to the left of the second and so on in zig-zag fashion, going around the last club. He returns to place in the same manner, starting the next player who does the same. If a player knocks down an Indian club, he must set it up before he continues.

DANCES

46. *Ace of Diamonds*

Record:
Victor-20989

Basic Steps

Polka; step-hop; skip.

FORMATION

Double circle is formed, partners facing, the girl being on the outside.

DANCE

Measures

1-4   Stamp right, stamp left, hook right elbows with your partner, and turn in circle with six skip steps.

5-8   Repeat 1-4, hooking left elbows.

9-16   Partners take four step-hops backward, moving away from each other. They repeat this, moving forward.

17-24   Face in the line of direction and join inside hands. Take eight polka steps forward. Turn to face your partner on the last polka step. Repeat all.

47. *American Quadrille*

Records:
Victor-20447A
(Money Musk)
Floyd Woodhull-36403
(Blackberry Quadrille)

BASIC STEPS

Allemande left; allemande right; do-si-do; grand right and left; right and left through.

FORMATION

Squares of eight are formed.

Dance

Measures

1-4   Do allemande left with corner, 8 counts.

5-8   Do allemande right with partner, 8 counts.

1-8   Head couples do right and left through and right and left back, 16 counts.

9-16   Do allemande left with corner, and allemande right with partner.

9-16   Side couples take right and left through and right and left back.

1-8   Do-si-do with your corner and a grand right and left. (Repeat music measures 1-8)

9-16   Do allemande left with corner and allemande right with partner.

9-16   The first and third couples join both hands with partner and exchange places with sliding steps. Then they return to place. 16 counts.

1-8   Do allemande left with corner and allemande right with partner.

1-8   The second and fourth couples exchange places with slide steps and return to place.

9-16   Do-si-do with your corner and do a grand right and left. (Repeat music measures 9-16)

1-8   Promenade with your partner.

1-8   Boys swing the corner girl and then swing their own partner.

48. *Csebogár*
(Hungarian)

Record:
Victor-20992

Basic Steps

Skip; Hungarian turn.

Formation

Partners stand in a single circle, facing the center. The girl is on the boy's right and all hands are joined.

Dance

Measures

1-8   Take eight skips to the right and eight skips to the left.

1-4   Take four skips to the center and four skips back to place.

5-8   Do a Hungarian turn. Partners stand with right sides together and place their right arm around each other's waist, raising the left arm overhead. They hop right, step left, step right. They repeat this three times, moving in a circle.

9-12   Partners are facing, hands joined. They slide the inside foot toward the center and close with the other. They repeat the same twice more. Then they take two stamps in place.

13-16   Repeat 9-12, starting with the outside foot, and move back to place.

9-10   Slide the inside foot toward the center, close with the other, slide the inside foot again, and stamp with the outside foot. Slide, close, slide, stamp.

11-12   Repeat starting with the outside foot and moving back to place.

13-16   Do a Hungarian turn.

49. *Donegal Country Dance*
(Irish)

BASIC STEPS

Slide; skip; promenade.

FORMATION

Partners stand in a single circle, facing the center. The girl is on the boy's right.

DANCE

Measures

1-8   All join hands and take eight slides to the right and eight slides to the left.

1-8   Repeat 1-8.

9-12   Give your right hand to your partner and turn once around with four skips. Turn, give the right hand to your neighbor, and turn once around with four skips.

13-16   Repeat 9-12, hooking elbows.

9-16   Promenade.

Repeat the dance, wherever you finish the promenade.

50. *Finnish Reel*
(Finnish)

BASIC STEPS

Skip; toe and heel.

FORMATION

Six or eight couples stand in two parallel lines, partners facing, with the hands on the hips.

Dance

Measures

1-4   Take four skips forward and four skips back to place.

5-8   Hop on the left foot and touch the right toe at the side, the toe being turned in and the heel up, count 1. Hop left again and touch the right heel at the side, the toe being turned up, count 2. Repeat hopping on the right foot. Alternate left and right feet. There are 8 counts.

9-10   Change places with your partner with four running steps. Start with the right foot.

11-12   Step to the right with the right foot, close the left foot to the right with a stamp, and clap hands at the same time. Repeat with step to the left and stamp to the right.

13-14   Repeat 9-10, changing back to place.

15-16   Repeat 11-12.

51. *Glow Worm*
(American)

Record:
Folkraft 11044*

Basic Steps

Schottische; step-hop; step-swing.

Formation

Double circle is formed, facing in the line of direction, left side being toward the center. The girl is on the boy's right and the inside hands are joined.

* Any 4/4 time music may be used.

DANCE

Measures

1-2   Take four walking steps forward, and then four steps returning to place.

3-4   Take four step-swings in place. Step right and swing your left foot across, pointing the toe. Repeat left, right, left.

5-8   Repeat 1-4.

9-12   Take four schottische steps forward. Start with the right foot and alternate.

13-14   Partners hold their inside hands high and the girl takes four step-hops, turning under the boy's arm.

15-16   Make a deep curtsey to your partner.

Repeat the dance with the boy turning under the girl's arm on measures 13-14.

52. *Heel and Toe Polka*

Record:
Henry Ford-107A

Basic Steps

Heel and toe polka ; polka.

Formation

Double circle is formed, with inside hands joined.

Dance

Part 1

Measures

A. 1-8   Starting with the outside foot, take four heel and toe polka steps forward.

B. 9-16   Take eight polka steps forward.

Part 2

A. 1-8   Repeat A of part 1.

B. 9-16   Take three polka steps forward and three stamps in place. Repeat the three polka steps and the three stamps.

Part 3

A. 1-8   Repeat A of part 1.

B. 9-16   Take eight polka steps forward. On the first

polka step, the partners turn to face each other and swing their joined inside hands backward. On the second polka step, the partners turn back to back and swing their arms forward. They alternate, turning face to face and back to back.

Part 4

A. 1-8   Repeat A of part 1.

B. 9-16   Take eight polka steps in social dance position.

53. *Highland Schottische*
(Scotch)

Record:
Victor-21616

BASIC STEPS

Highland step; schottische; running schottische.

FORMATION

Partners facing in two parallel lines.

DANCE

Part 1

Measures

1   Take one highland step right. Hop on the left foot and touch the right toe to the side. Hop on the left foot **again**, bringing the right toe behind the left knee. Repeat the hop, bringing the right toe in front.

2   Take one schottische step right.

3-4   Repeat 1-2 to the left.

1-4   Repeat 1-4.

5-8　　Change places with the opposite dancer with four running schottische steps.

Part 2

Repeat all of part 1, but return to your own place on measures 5-8.

Repeat the dance several times.

54. *Hinky-Dinky, Parlee-Voo*
(American)

The following singing call can also be used:

Head two ladies go forward and back, Parlee-Voo.
Forward again and do-si-do, Parlee-Voo.
Allemande left on the corner all,
And do-si-do with partners all, Hinky-Dinky, Parlee-
    Voo.

Promenade around the hall, Parlee-Voo.
Follow the one ahead of you, Parlee-Voo.
Allemande left on the corner all,
And turn your partner once for all, Hinky-Dinky, Par-
    lee-Voo.

BASIC STEPS

Allemande left; do-si-do; promenade.

FORMATION

Squares of eight are formed.

DANCE

Measures

1-4   Head ladies walk four steps forward and clap
hands on the fourth step. They walk four steps backward and all
sing: "Parlee-Voo." *

5-8   Head ladies walk forward and do-si-do, and all
sing: "Parlee-Voo" on measures 7 and 8.

9-12   Do allemande left on the corner.

13-16   Do-si-do with partner and all sing: "Hinky-
Dinky, Parlee-Voo."

1-8   All promenade.

9-12   Do allemande on the corner.

* Each time the phrase: "Parlee-Voo" or "Hinky-Dinky, Parlee-
Voo" appears in the music everyone sings it.

13-16   Swing your partner.

The two side ladies repeat the action of the two head ladies. Then the two head gents and two side gents do the same. In between each figure, there is a promenade, allemande left, and swing your partner as above.

55. *Irish Washerwoman*
(American)

Record :

Victor-21616

BASIC STEPS

Allemande left; do-si-do; right and left through; ladies chain.

FORMATION

Squares of eight are formed.

D<small>ANCE</small>

Measures

1-8   Join hands and take eight slides right and eight slides left.

9-16   Take four skips toward the center and four skips back. Repeat.

1-8   Head couples do right and left through and right and left back.

9-16   Side couples repeat 1-8.

1-8   Take allemande left on the corner and do-si-do with your partner.

9-16   Head ladies make chain across and back.

1-8   Side ladies repeat.

9-16   Take allemande left on the corner and do-si-do with your partner.

1-8   Do a grand right and left.

9-16   Gents swing the corner lady, then swing their partner.

1-8   They promenade with their partner.

9-16   They swing the corner lady and then their partner.

56. *Kalvelis*

(Lithuanian)

Records:

Folkraft 1051A

Folkraft M-301

B<small>ASIC</small> S<small>TEP</small>

Polka.

FORMATION

. Partners are in a single circle, facing the center. The girl is on the boy's right and all hands are joined.

DANCE

Part 1

Measures

A. 1-8   Take seven polka steps to the right and then three stamps.

1-8   Repeat to the left.

B. 9-16   Clap hands four times. Place your right hand on top of the left, then turn your hands and place the left hand on top of the right. Alternate right and left hands.

11-12   Hook right elbows and turn with four skips.

13-16   Hook left elbows and repeat 11-12.

9-16   Repeat all of 9-16.

Part 2

A. 1-8   In a double circle, partners facing in the line of direction, take three polka steps forward and three stamps in place. They repeat the three polka steps and the three stamps.

1-8   Repeat 1-8 of part 2 A.

B. Repeat all of B in part 1 (9-16 twice).

Part 3

A. 1-8   Face the center of the circle, take three polka steps to the center and three stamps. Turn on the stamps and

return to your place with three polka steps and three stamps.
Turn to face the center on the stamps.

    1-8   Repeat 1-8 of part 3.

    B. Repeat all of B in part 1.

Part 4

    A. 1-8   Take sixteen free polka steps. Dance polka
with your partner any place around the room. (Repeat music
measures 1-8.)

    B. Repeat all of B in part 1 wherever you are on the floor.
Repeat part 4 as many times as desired.

57. *Polka Couple Dance*

Record:

Any polka music*

*If a record is used, select one with moderate tempo.

BASIC STEP

   Polka.

FORMATION

   Double circle is formed. Partners are facing the line of direction with their left side toward the center. The girl is on the boy's right, the inside hands being joined.

DANCE

   Measures

   1-8   Starting on the outside foot, take five polka steps forward. Then turn away from your partner in a small circle with two polka steps. End facing your partner with three stamps.

   1-8   Repeat 1-8.

9-12   Each starting right, take one polka step to the right side, and tap the left toe three times to the floor.

13-16   Partners join and hold high their right hands. Partners turn with three polka steps so that they are in opposite places. They make three stamps in place.

9-12   Repeat 9-12 in the new place.

13-16   Repeat 13-16, returning to your own place.

58. *Rakes of Mallow* (*Waves of Tory*)
(Irish)

Record:
Folkraft-33505F

Basic Steps

Right and left-hand star; promenade.

Formation

Dancers form six or eight couples in two parallel lines, partners facing.

Dance

Measures

1-4   Take four steps forward and four back to place. Repeat.

5-6   Go forward again. The first couple and the second couple join right hands and walk eight steps in circle, making the right-hand star. The remaining couples do the same. (8 counts)

7-8   Turn, join the left hands, and walk in opposite direction, forming a left-hand star. (8 counts)

1-8   Face the head of the set and join hands with your partner. The head couple turns right and leads the whole set directly back to the foot of the set. Then it returns to place.

1-4   The lines are facing each other. The gents of the first couple and the second couple join inside hands and raise them high. The ladies of the first couple and the second couple join right hands, but keep them low. The ladies and gents change places with eight steps. The ladies go under the arch made by the gents. Then they return to place with the gents going under the arch made by the ladies. The remaining four couples do the same.

5-8   Repeat 1-4.

1-8   The head couple joins hands, turns right and goes to the foot of the set. The other couples follow. The head couple forms an arch and the others pass under.

The dance is repeated with a new head couple. When forming the right-hand star, each couple will have a new couple to dance with.

59. *Sailor's Hornpipe*
(English)

Record:
Victor-21685

BASIC STEPS

Polka; single pigeon toe.

FORMATION

Single lines are formed.

DANCE

Measures

A. 1-4   Take six polka steps, turning in a small circle to the right. Take three steps in place and hold the fourth count. Fold your arms and raise them shoulder high.

5-8   Repeat 1-4, turning to the left.

B. 9-12   Sight land by looking to the right, and shading the eyes with the right hand and doing a single pigeon toe to the right. (Turn the right heel outward, pivot on the right toe, count 1. Turn the right toe outward, pivot on the right heel, count 2. Continue moving toward the right side, dragging the left foot.) This takes sixteen counts.

13-16   Repeat 9-12, moving in the opposite direction for twelve counts. Take three stamps in place.

C. 1-3   Hitch your trousers. Place the right hand in front, waist high, and the left hand on the back, palm up. Slide diagonally forward to the right on the right foot and hop on the right foot three times.

Repeat with the left foot, moving to the left. Change the position of your hands, left in front and right in back.

Repeat to the right again.

4   Take three steps in place, holding the fourth count.

5-8   Repeat measures 1-4. Stamp three times on the eighth measure.

D. 9   Pull up anchor. Leap forward on the left foot and grasp an imaginary rope; then step back on the right foot and pull up the rope.

10   Run backward four small steps, pulling the rope.

11-16   Repeat measure 9-10 **twice**. On measure 15, leap forward and step back as before, but substitute three stamps for the running steps on measure 16.

60. *Schottische Hop*

Record:
Folkraft F117B
(Military Schottische)

Basic Steps

Schottische; step-hop.

Formation

Six or eight couples stand in two parallel lines. Partners are facing, the back of their hands on the hips.

Dance

Measures

1-2   Take one schottische step right and one left.

3-4   Take four step-hops in place.

5-8   Repeat 1-4.

9-10   Repeat 1-2.

11-12   Take four step-hops, changing places with your partner, passing right shoulders.

13-14   Repeat 1-2.

15-16   Repeat 11-12, moving back to your own place.

1-8   Repeat.

9-10   Take one schottische step right and one left.

11-12   Hook right elbows and take four step-hops in circle, returning to your own place.

13-16   Repeat 9-12.

61. *Sellenger's Round*
(English)

Record:
Victor-20445B

BASIC STEPS

Set and turn single; a double.

FORMATION

Partners stand in a single circle, facing center. The girl is on the boy's right and all hands are joined.

DANCE

Part 1

Measures

A. 1-8   Take eight slides to the right and eight slides to the left.

B. 9-12   Drop the hands, take a double to the center, and clap hands on the fourth step. Move back to place with four steps and clap.

13-16   Partners set and turn single.

9-16   Repeat.

Part 2

A. 1-4   Girls walk four steps toward the center and four steps back to place.

5-8   Boys repeat this.

B. Repeat all of B in part 1.

Part 3

A. 1-8   Partners face and change places, passing left shoulders and taking four steps. They return to place, passing right shoulders.

B. Repeat all of B in part 1.

Part 4

A. 1-8   Partners hook right elbows and turn once around, taking four steps. They repeat this, hooking left elbows.

B. Repeat all of B in part 1.

62. *Sicilian Circle*
(American)

Records:
Victor-22991-20639
Floyd Woodhull-36403
(Blackberry Quadrille)

BASIC STEPS

Do-si-do; ladies chain.

FORMATION

Partners are in a double circle. Every other couple faces in opposite direction, making sets of four in a large circle.

DANCE

Measures (Two counts to each measure)

1-4   Take four steps forward and four steps back to place.

5-8   Each set of four joins hands in a circle and takes four steps to the right and four steps to the left.

9-16   Gents do-si-do with opposite lady, then do-si-do with their partner.

1-8   Ladies chain over and back.

9-12   Take four steps toward each other and four steps back to place.

13-16   Take four steps forward again and pass through to meet a new couple.

Repeat the dance with the new couple and continue as many times as desired.

63. *Skater's Schottische*

BASIC STEPS

Schottische; step-hop.

FORMATION

Double circle is formed, facing in the line of direction; hands are crossed in skaters' position. The girl is on the outside.

DANCE

Measures

1-4   Take one schottische step to the right and one to the left. Repeat to right and left.

5-8   Take four schottische steps, moving forward. Partners face on the last schottische step.

1-4   Move away from your partner with one schottische step to the right. Move back to place with one schottische step to the left. Repeat to right and left.

5-8   Cross your hands in skating position and take eight step-hops, turning in a circle.

Repeat all several times.

64. The Hatter
(Danish)

Record:
Victor-20449

BASIC STEPS

Slide; promenade; skip.

FORMATION

Partners are in a single circle, facing center. The girl is on the boy's right. Squares of eight may also be used.

Dance

Part 1

Measures

A. 1-8   Take eight slides right.

1-8   Repeat eight slides left.

B. 9-16   Partners facing, stamp three times and hold the fourth count. Clap hands three times and hold the fourth count. Repeat stamping and clapping, facing your neighbor.

9-16   Repeat 9-16.

17-24   Promenade with partner, sixteen skips.

(repeat)

Part 2

A. 1-8   Girls step just inside the circle, join hands in a circle, and take eight slides to the right.

1-8   Repeat eight slides to the left.

B. 9-24   Repeat all of B in part 1.

Part 3

A. 1-8   Repeat all of A in part 2, with the boys joining hands in a circle.

(repeat)

B. 9-24   Repeat all of B in part 1.

Part 4

A. 1-8   Hook right elbows with your neighbor and turn once around with eight skips.

1-8   Repeat, hooking elbows with your partner.

B. 9-24   Repeat all of B in part 1.

65. *Turkey in the Straw*
(American)

Record:
Victor-22131

Basic Steps

Do-si-do, allemande left; grand right and left.

Formation

Squares of eight are formed.

Dance

Part 1

Measures

1-8   All join hands and take eight slides to the right and eight slides to the left.

9-16   Gents swing the corner lady, then swing their partner.

Part 2

1-4   The first two couples take four steps toward each other and four steps returning to place.

5-8   The first couple leads to the second couple with four steps, join hands with them and they take four steps in circle to the right.

9-16   Gents swing the opposite lady and then they swing their own partner.

The first couple repeats part 2 with the third couple and then with the fourth couple.

Part 3

1-16   Do-si-do with your partner, then allemande left with the corner, and take a grand right and left.

Repeat part 2 with the second couple leading. Then repeat with the third couple and the fourth couple. In between each figure do part 3.

SELF-TESTING ACTIVITIES

66. *Ankle Toss*

Place a ball or bean bag between the ankles and, by jumping, toss the ball upward far enough to be able to catch it with the hands.

67. *Chair Dip*

Place the back of a straight chair or a small bench against a wall. Grasp the outside edges of the chair seat with the hands and extend the legs out in back so that the weight is on the hands and toes. Bend the elbows so that the chest touches the front edge of the chair or bench and then straighten the elbows. Keep the body straight. Repeat this as many times as possible.

68. *Heel Jump*

Take a squat position on the floor with your arms folded across the chest and your weight on the toes. Spring to a standing position, placing the weight on the heels with the toes up, flinging the arms upward. Repeat this several times in rapid succession. Try to move forward a little each time.

69. *Hop Contest*

Take a piece of chalk and stand on one foot on a starting line. Take one hop forward and mark a line on the floor, in front of the foot carrying the weight. Hop forward again on the same foot, marking the distance as before. Hop four times. Compare all marks to see which of the contestants could hop farthest from the starting line. If a player loses his balance and touches the floor with his free foot or either hand, he must start again.

70. *Human Arch*

Lie with your back on a mat and place one hand on each side of the head with palms down and fingers pointing toward the shoulders. Bend the knees and place the feet as close to the body as possible. Push up with your hands so that the weight rests on the hands and toes. Arch the body as much as possible. Try to walk forward in this position by moving the right hand and right foot and then the left hand and left foot.

71. *Jump the Stick*

Hold a stick or wand in front with both hands. Jump over the stick without releasing either hand. If successful, try jumping back. Hold the stick lightly with the finger tips to avoid the danger of tripping.

72. *Midget Walk*

Kneel on both knees on a mat and raise the heels grasping the ankles with the hands. In this position, walk forward.

73. *Monkey Roll*

The first child lies on his back on a mat, with the hands close to his head, and raises the feet upward, legs apart. The second child stands with one foot on each side of his partner's head. The first child grasps the ankles of the second child who leans forward and grasps the ankles of the first child.

The second child springs forward, tucks his head and does a forward roll between his part-ner's legs. As the second child rolls over, he brings the first child to a standing position. The stunt is repeated with the first child rolling this time. It is important that each child keeps a firm grasp on his partner's ankles and the roll is forceful enough to pull the partner up.

74. *Mule Kick*

From a standing position, take a little jump and place your hands on the floor quickly. Just as the hands touch the floor, kick the feet out backward. When the feet drop to the floor, push up with the hands and come to a partial standing position. Repeat this several times in rapid succession.

75. *Novelty Walk*

Sit on the floor and place the weight on your hands and feet. Keep the body straight. Walk in this position by lifting the left foot and the left hand. Before the left hand touches the floor again, slap the left side of your body with your hand. Repeat, moving the right foot and the right hand. Travel a designated distance.

76. *Seal Slap*

Take a squat position on the floor and extend your legs back. Lift your hands from the floor, clap them together once, and put them back in the original position.

77. *Single Leg Squat*

Stand with the weight on the left foot. Bend the right knee and grasp the right toe with the left hand. Extend the right leg and bend the supporting leg to a squat position. In this position, keep the balance without using the left hand for support. Return to a starting position. Repeat with the weight on the right foot.

78. *Sitting Balance*

The first player lies on his back on a mat and bends his knees to his chest with the feet parallel to the floor, soles turned up. The second player, with his back toward the first, sits on the first player's feet. The first player straightens his legs and pushes the second player to a sitting balance position. The second player should keep his legs out straight and raise his arms sideward for balance.

79. *Tandem*

The first player stands behind the second. The first player bends his knees and the second player sits on the first player's knees. In this position, they walk forward, both moving first the right foot and then the left. Several people may form a line to carry out the action. The line is held together by placing the hands on the hips of the player in front.

80. *Team Forward Rolls*

Three people line up at the edge of a mat and do a forward roll at the same time. They turn around and do another roll returning to place. Attempts should be made to get perfect timing so that each starts and finishes at the same time. It is important that the rolls are straight.

81. *Toe Kick*

Stand with the weight on both feet. Jump and raise both feet upward. Touch the toes with your hands.

82. *Wall Push*

Stand, facing a wall at a distance of about two or three feet. Place the left hand behind the back and the right hand against the wall. Push to an upright position. Repeat this several times, increasing the distance each time.

83. Bull Fight

Two players are on their hands and knees on a mat. Each moves around in this position and attempts to push his opponent over or force him off the mat. The hands must not be removed from the mat at any time. If a mat is not available, mark off a similar area on the floor.

84. Club Fight

Two players stand in a circle about six feet in diameter. An Indian club is placed in the center. Each player stands on his right foot and grasps his left foot with the left hand. They hop around, trying to grasp the club. The player who is forced out of the circle or loses his balance before the contest is ended is eliminated. The player who is left takes on a new opponent. This continues until someone secures the club.

85. Finger Pull

Two players stand facing each other. One bends his elbows and hooks his fingers together in front of him. The other grasps his opponent's wrists and attempts to pull his fingers apart.

86. Hand Wrestle

Two players stand facing each other and placing the outside of their right feet side by side, with the left feet back for balance. The right hands are joined as each attempts to push his opponent so that he loses his balance and moves one or both feet from the floor. Players are not allowed to push with the body.

87. *Rooster Fight*

Two players stand in a circle about five or six feet in diameter. Each takes a squat position and folds his arms across his chest. In this position, each player moves around and attempts to make the other lose his balance or force him out of the circle.

88. *Stick Pull*

Two players sit on the floor, facing each other and placing the soles of their feet together. Each grasps a stick with his hands and tries to pull the other up. The player who is pulled off the floor, loses his balance, or releases the stick loses the contest.

89. *Stick Wrestle*

Two players stand facing each other, grasping a stick or wand with both hands. Each player attempts to turn the stick and touch the floor on his right side with one end of the stick.

Grade Six

This is the beginning of the transitional period between childhood and early adolescence. There is a noticeable spurt of growth especially for girls. The girls are usually taller and heavier than the boys, but are starting to fall behind in physical strength and endurance. There may be signs of awkwardness at this age if the skeletal growth and muscular development are out of proportion.

Along with increasing power to concentrate, children are making progress in the ability to reason. They are also beginning to have a deeper insight into situations and are capable of better judgment.

The desire for more highly organized games enhances the competitive spirit on a team basis. There is also a growing respect for good sportsmanship. Leadership is more highly developed. Membership in clubs or organizations sponsored by the school or community is of growing importance. A desire to participate in local "drives" for the benefit of these organizations or other worthy causes is manifest. Boys and girls still prefer to play separately, but are slowly developing a social consciousness which is displayed by their interest in mixed group activities, such as square dancing.

SUGGESTED LESSON PLANS

September

Activities	Equipment	Section
GAMES		
Football Skills	Several balls	11
Mass Soccer	One ball	19
Fifty-One or Bust	Some old rubber heels	10
Squeeze-Out		25
DANCES		
Cracoviac	Folkraft Record F1102	46
Push the Business on		56
Shoo Fly		58
SELF-TESTING ACTIVITIES		
Toe Lift	A small rubber ball or other object	83
Siamese Hop		77

October

Activities	Equipment	Section
GAMES		
Touch Football Tag	One ball	27
Punt Ball	One ball, four bases	22
Double Dodge Ball	One ball	7
RELAYS		
Soccer Kick Relay	One ball for each team	40
Jump the Ditch Relay		36
DANCES		
Rheinlander		57
Skip to My Lou	Folkraft Record F1103	59
The Shamrock	Victor Record 21616A	66
	Decca Record 3000A	
SELF-TESTING ACTIVITIES		
Balance Bend	A piece of chalk	70
Head Push		91

November

Activities	Equipment	Section
GAMES		
Three Shots	A wastebasket or box and a ball for each team	26
Wide Awake	A ball	30
RELAYS		
Bowling Relay	One ball for each team	31
Steady Hand Relay	Two pennies for each team	41
DANCES		
Arkansas Traveler	Victor Record 20638	43
Bavarian Dance		45
The Circle with Six	Victor Record 22991	63
SELF-TESTING ACTIVITIES		
Tight-Rope Walk	A ruler or a book	82
Wall Hop		86

December

Activities	Equipment	Section
GAMES		
Guard Ball	One ball	12
Jump the Shot	A bean bag and a rope	16
RELAYS		
Handy Feet Relay	One Indian club and one chair for each team	33
Hobble Race Relay		34
DANCES		
Oxford Minuet	Decca Record 2091B Decca Record 25059	53
Pass the Shoe		54
SELF-TESTING ACTIVITIES		
Elbow Dip	A piece of paper	74
Wooden Man		85

January

Activities	Equipment	Section
GAMES		
Circle Keep Up	One volley ball or light-weight ball for each team	6
Hustle Hustle		14
One Less	A collection of objects, such as, chalk, erasers, etc.	20
RELAYS		
Human Croquet Relay		35
Obstacle Hop Relay	One bean bag for each team	37
DANCES		
Army and Navy Dance	Victor record 20190	44
Norwegian Mountain March	Victor record 20151	51
The Black Nag		62
SELF-TESTING ACTIVITIES		
Couple Bear Dance		73
Triple Rolls	A mat	84
Bull Dog Pull		87

February

Activities	Equipment	Section
GAMES		
Drive Ball	One ball	9
Center Miss Ball	Two balls	5
Balloon Ball	Balloons or a light-weight ball	1
RELAYS		
One-Hand Pass Relay	One ball for each team	38
Quartet Relay		39
DANCES		
Military Two-Step	Decca Record 2091A	47
The Wild Irishman	Victor Record 21616	67
Weaving Cloth	Victor Record 21616B Part 2	69
SELF-TESTING ACTIVITIES		
Thigh Balance		81
Skin the Snake		78
Champion of the Ring		88

March

Activities	Equipment	Section
GAMES		
Lickety Split		17
Dribble Ball	One ball	8
RELAYS		
Couple Slide Relay		32
Swing Your Partner Relay		42
DANCES		
Money Musk	Victor Record 20447A	48
New Century Hornpipe	Victor Record 20592A	50
Waltz Quadrille	Any Waltz Record	68
SELF-TESTING ACTIVITIES		
Back to Back Pull Over		71
Kangaroo Fight	A bean bag or newspaper	92
Hand Push		90

April

Activities	Equipment	Section
GAMES		
Poison Pin	Three Indian clubs	21
Triangle Run		28
Jump Rope	Individual jump ropes and long ropes	15
DANCES		
Southern Schottische	Ford Record 103B	60
Swedish Varsouvianna		61
SELF-TESTING ACTIVITIES		
Spinning Wheel		79
Flying Angel	A mat	75
Crane Wrestle		89

May

Activities	Equipment	Section
GAMES		
Bunt Baseball	One softball or baseball, one bat, four bases	4
Line-Up Ball	One ball, four bases	18
Beat Ball	One ball, four bases	3
Hop Scotch	A stone	13
Ladder		
Finland		
Pick Up		
Italian		
Tournament		
Snail		
DANCES		
Multiplication Dance		49
O' Susie	Folkraft Record 1017A Victor Record 20638A	52
The Rye Waltz	Ford Record 107B Folkraft Record 1044	65
SELF-TESTING ACTIVITIES		
Merry-Go-Round		76
Knee Wrestle		93

June

Activities	Equipment	Section
GAMES		
Baseball Twenty-One	One softball, one bat, four bases	2
Roley-Hop	One small ball	23
Twenty-Five Yard Dash	A watch with a second hand or a stop watch	29
Standing Broad Jump	Measuring tape	24
DANCES		
Paul Jones	Any good march record	55
The Hesitation Waltz	Any good waltz record	64
SELF-TESTING ACTIVITIES		
Caterpillar Walk		72
Stick Twist	A stick	80

GAMES

1. *Balloon Ball*

Equipment : Balloons or light-weight ball.

FORMATION

Players are scattered around the room.

ACTION

A balloon or ball is tossed into the group of players who tap or volley the balloon, trying to work it to an end wall. The player who succeeds in touching the end wall with the balloon earns one point for himself. No player may hold the balloon. If the balloon hits the floor, the leader tosses it into the air again from that spot. It will be well to have several inflated balloons handy to replace broken ones.

VARIATION

There are two equal teams, each team attempting to work the ball to opposite end walls. The team that succeeds, scores one point. A total of five points completes one game.

2. *Baseball Twenty-One*

Equipment : One softball or baseball and a bat, four bases.

FORMATION

The field and the players are arranged as in softball. There is one scorer for each team.

ACTION

The game is played in the same manner as softball, except that a runner receives a point for each base he touches without being put out. The team first making twenty-one points wins.

Scoring

Out at first	No point
Out at second	1 point
Out at third	2 points
Out at home	3 points
Home Run	4 points

NOTE

A batter must hit the ball in order to advance to first base in this game. He cannot be awarded a base on four balls.

3. *Beat Ball*

Equipment : One ball, four bases.

FORMATION

There are two equal teams, one at bat and the other in the field. The field is marked in the same manner as for softball. One field player is on each base, the rest of the players being scattered in the field. The team at bat lines up at home plate.

ACTION

The player at bat throws a fair ball anywhere in the field. He then tries to run all the bases before the ball is thrown around the bases by the opposing team. If the ball makes the rounds of the bases first, the runner is out. Each baseman must touch his base while he has the ball. A fly ball caught puts the runner out. When there are three outs the teams change places. As the ball is thrown into the field, the fielders relay the ball to first base, then to second, to third and to home. If the runner beats the ball, he scores a point for his team.

4. *Bunt Baseball*

This game is useful in a crowded play area to play baseball.

Equipment: One softball or baseball, one bat, and four bases.

FORMATION

The playing area is a small baseball diamond. No outfield area is needed. The players are the same as for baseball except there are no outfielders. One team is at bat and the other is in the field.

ACTION

The game is played like baseball except that the batters must "bunt." * A player is out if he swings the bat, whether he hits the

* To properly execute a bunt, the batter grasps the bat with one hand near the end and slides the other hand down the bat near the trade mark. The bat is out in front of his body and parallel to the ground. The player meets the ball with the bat in this position without swinging the bat.

ball or not. When there are three outs, the teams change places.

5. *Center Miss Ball*

Equipment: Two balls.

FORMATION

Players stand in circle, with a player in the center.

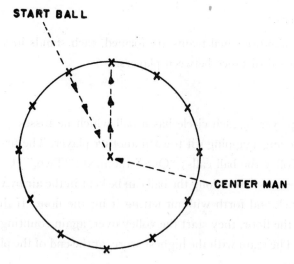

ACTION

One player standing in the circle and the center player has a ball. On a signal, the circle player throws his ball to the center player, while the center player throws his to the player standing on the left of the circle player who started the ball.

The two balls are kept moving in and out until the center player misses. When the center misses, he changes places with the circle player who threw the pass.

This game provides an excellent opportunity to teach accurate chest passing.

VARIATION

After this skill has been developed, use the bounce pass, two-hand under hand, one-hand underhand, and two-hand overhead passes.

6. *Circle Keep Up*

Equipment : One volley ball or light rubber ball for each team.

FORMATION

Two or more equal teams are formed, each stands in a circle with a good distance between players.

ACTION

One player in each circle has a ball which he tosses into the air, volleying (tapping) it toward another player. The first person to volley the ball calls: "One," the next: "Two," etc. Each team tries to see how long the ball can be kept in the air by volleying it back and forth without letting it hit the floor. If the ball touches the floor, they start the volley over, again counting from "One." The team with the highest score, at the end of the playing time wins.

7. *Double Dodge Ball*

Equipment: One ball.

FORMATION

Two opposing teams are playing in three areas. One team plays in the center area, the other team divides in half and plays in the two end areas.

X TEAM A
O TEAM B

ACTION

The players in the end areas try to eliminate the players in the center by hitting them below the waist with the ball. The center players evade the ball as in regular dodge ball. If the ball comes to a stop in the center area, a player from the end area may go and get it. However he must return to his own area before he may throw the ball at an opponent.

After a set time of play, or when all the center players are eliminated, the teams change playing areas. The team that has eliminated the greater number of players, at the end of the playing time, is the winner.

8. *Dribble Ball*

Equipment: One ball.

FORMATION

The play area is divided in half. A three-foot circle is drawn about five feet from each end line. There are two equal teams, one half of each team playing guard; the other half playing forward. This activity is excellent to develop skill in the pivot, bounce pass, and dribble.

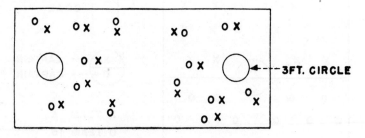

X TEAM A
O TEAM B

ACTION

The ball is tossed at center between two opposing players. Each one tries to tap it to one of his forwards. The ball is moved around the court by the pivot and pass, bounce pass, or the dribble; no other pass may be used. A point is made when a forward can bounce the ball in his own circle, which is guarded by all the opposing guards in that half of the court. Other basketball rules are followed; a foul is called when anyone catches a pass other than those named previously. After a foul, the ball is given to an opponent for a free throw at his opponents' goal. No player may step over the center line and no guard may step into his own circle.

9. *Drive Ball*

Equipment : One ball and a watch or timer.

FORMATION

An area, about the size of a basketball court, is needed. There are two equal teams with one "Captain" and one "Goalkeeper,

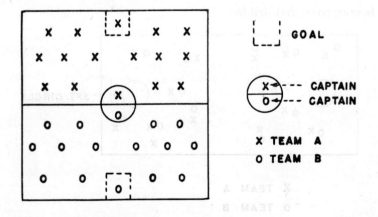

for each. One player is the scorer. The players are scattered and assigned to a definite position. They may play within a two foot area around their assigned position, but nowhere else. Circles, two feet in diameter, may be drawn on the floor to mark their places.

ACTION

The ball is put in play by a toss between the two Captains. It is kept in play by being thrown from one court to the other. Each team tries to throw the ball in the opponents' goal. If they succeed, they score two points for their team. In defending his goal, the Goalkeeper may not step out of his territory.

It is a foul to kick the ball, hold the ball, cross the center line, or to step more than two feet away from a player's assigned position. Each foul gives one point to the opponents' team. This game may be played in two periods, the length of play being determined before the start of the game. The teams change sides at the end of each period.

10. *Fifty-One or Bust*

Equipment: Ask your local shoemaker for some old rubber heels that are about the same size and weight.

FORMATION

Two to six players may play on one diagram. Each player has one rubber heel. Mark the diagrams on the sidewalk, ground, or floor.

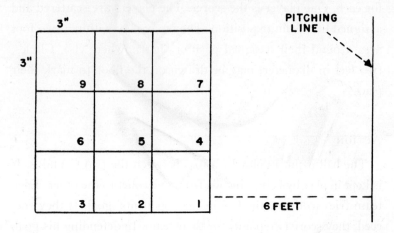

ACTION

The players take turns, tossing the heels on the target. Any that land on the line or outside, do not count. The points are added as they go. The player who reaches a total of fifty-one points first wins. Should a player score over fifty-one points, he "busts" and must restart with a zero score.

11. *Football Skills*

GRIPPING THE BALL

Stand the ball on end in the left hand, and, with the right hand, grasp the ball slightly above the center on the lacing. Spread the fingers slightly and extend the thumb around the ball.

CENTERING THE BALL

Put the ball in play either by passing or by handing it back between the legs.

PUNT

Hold the ball with the hands, then kick it before it touches the ground. Hold it pointed obliquely away from the kicking foot and kick it with the instep, not the toe.

DROP KICK

Drop the ball point first on the ground, and then kick it a little below the middle, with the toe.

PLACE KICK

Kick the ball with the toe from a fixed position on the ground. Often a tee is used or the ball is held by another player.

12. *Guard Ball*

Equipment: One ball.

FORMATION

Two parallel lines, about ten feet apart, are drawn in the center of the play area. There are two equal teams. One team

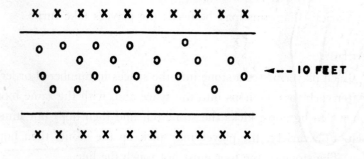

plays between the two parallel lines. The other team, divided in half, plays outside the lines, half on each side. There is one scorer and one timer.

ACTION

The line team tries to pass the ball back and forth over the center players, as in basketball. The center team guards the opposing players near the line and tries to intercept the passes. A completed pass over the team in the center counts one point. If the ball is blocked or intercepted by the center team, it is started again by the line team.

The play continues for four three-minute periods. Teams change places after each period. At the end of the playing time, the team that has made more passes wins.

13. *Hop Scotch*

Equipment: A stone.

FORMATION

Various diagrams may be used; the players take turns.

ACTION

Each player tosses a stone into the spaces in numbered order. After each toss, he hops into the space and, with the same foot on which he hops, kicks the stone out and then hops out himself. For variety, the player may pick up the stone, then hop out. The stone or the foot must not touch the line.

VARIATIONS

Ladder Hop Scotch

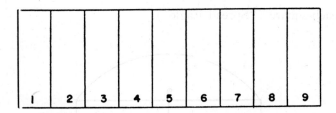

1. *Hop It.* The player starts on one foot. He tosses the stone into space 1, hops over space 1 into space 2. He picks up the stone and hops out via space 1. Next, he tosses the stone into space 2, hops over space 2, into space 3. Picking up the stone, he hops into space 2, space 1, and out. He continues up the ladder, then down the ladder.

2. *Kick It.* The procedure is the same as for "Hop It," except that the player hops into the the square with the stone. He kicks the stone out rather than pick it up.

3. *Up and Back.* The same method as with the others, except that the player tosses into space 1, hops over space 1 and on up to space 9, then back. He picks up the stone on the way back and hops out.

4. *Misses.* A player misses when:

   1. The stone falls in the wrong number.

   2. The stone or his foot hits any line.

   3. He hops in the block when the stone is there.

   4. His fingers or body touch the ground.

   5. He fails to hop over the stone.

Finland Hop Scotch

Toss the stone into space 1. Hop into space 1, pick up the stone, and hop out. Toss the stone into space 2. Hop into space

1, then into space 2. Pick up the stone and hop out. Continue up and back. In spaces 4, 5, 7, and 8, both feet may touch, one in each square ("Spread Eagle").

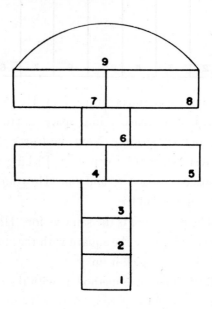

A player misses by touching lines, using two feet in other than allowed squares and changing feet.

Pick Up Hop Scotch

The stone is always tossed into the center block. First, player tosses the stone into the center, hops into block 1, picks up the stone, and hops out. He then tosses the stone into the center, hops into block 1, then into block 2. He picks up the stone and hops out via block 1. He continues advancing from block to block, always tossing to the center from the block just before the one in which he is to stop to pick up the stone.

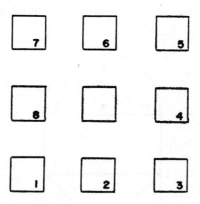

Italian Hop Scotch

Toss the stone into space 1. Hop into space 1, kick the stone into space 2, then into space 3 and on into space 8. In space 8, both feet may be put down. Pick up the stone, and hop out. Continue backwards, from space 8 to space 1, in the same manner.

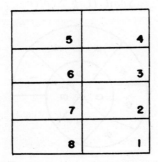

Tournament Hop Scotch

The stone is kicked as many times as necessary to move it from number to number. It is a miss if it lands on a line. A double foot landing may be used in areas number 1 & 2, 4 & 5, and both feet may land in area number 7.

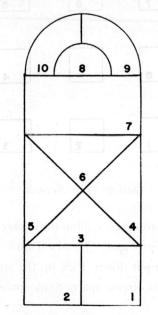

Snail Hop Scotch

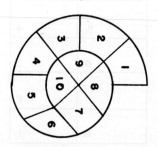

This is played the same way as regular Hop Scotch.

14. *Hustle, Hustle*

FORMATION

Two equal teams are formed, each player being lined up behind a captain in a straight line. Each player should mark his spot on the floor.

ACTION

On a signal, everyone leaves his spot and wanders any place he chooses. On another signal, they run for their own places. The team first returning in perfect order wins.

15. *Jump Rope*

1. Use individual rope turned by the jumper.
   a. Swing the rope forward over the head and under the feet.
   b. Swing the rope backward over the head and under the feet.
   c. Individual jumping may be done with one foot, two feet, hopping, stepping, running, and cross arm.
   d. Two people jump as they stand side by side, each holding one end of the rope.
   e. Two people jump as they stand face to face or back to back.
2. Use long rope turned by two people.
   a. The jumper starts standing in the middle or:
      (1) Runs in, jumps, runs out.
      (2) Runs in, jumps several times in succession, runs out.
      (3) Runs in and drops an object, jumps, picks it up, and runs out.
   b. The jumper skips through the long rope, swinging an individual jump rope.

16. *Jump the Shot*

Equipment: One bean bag tied to the end of a rope.

FORMATION

Players are in a single circle. One player with the rope and bean bag stands in the center.

ACTION

The center player swings the rope close to the floor near the players' feet. As the rope circles, the players jump to avoid being touched. If the bean bag or rope touches a player, he is eliminated.

17. *Lickety Split*

FORMATION

Two equal teams are lined up about fifteen feet apart. The players are numbered from opposite ends. One player is the "Caller" and scorer.

ACTION

The Caller calls any number he chooses. For example, he calls, "Number Four." The two Number Fours run and meet in the center. Here they must do "Peas Porridge Hot" (slap knees, own hands, then partner's hands) three times, then run "Lickety Split" * for home. The runner reaching his place first scores one point for his team. The team with more points wins.

The Caller must be sure to use all the numbers to give everyone a turn. He may also repeat the numbers.

* "Lickety Split" means run as fast as you can.

18. *Line-Up Ball*

Equipment : One ball.

FORMATION

A softball diamond is used. There are two equal teams, one is at bat and the other in the field, with an umpire and a scorer.

ACTION

The first player kicks the ball out into the field and tries to run the bases back to home plate. The fielder who recovers the ball, holds it up over his head while all the fielders line up behind him. If the fielders get lined up before the runner crosses home plate, the runner is out. If the runner makes the rounds first, he scores one run for his team. A fly ball caught puts a runner out. After three outs the teams change places. The team with more runs, after an equal number of times at bat, wins.

VARIATION

Use a playground ball and a bat.

19. *Mass Soccer*

Equipment : One soccer ball and a whistle.

FORMATION

The field is the same as for soccer, except that the goal lines are the goals. No goal posts, goal areas, or penalty areas are used.

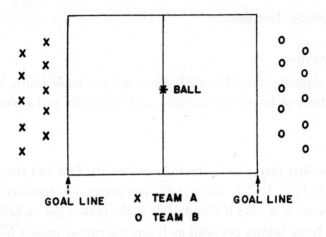

GOAL LINE   X   TEAM A   GOAL LINE

O   TEAM B

ACTION

The teams line up behind their goal lines. The ball is placed in the center of the field. At the whistle, the players rush the ball and attempt to kick it down to, and over, the opponents' goal line. If a team is successful, one point is scored. The ball is returned to the center after each goal. A game consists of two five-minute playing periods.

RULES

1. A free kick is awarded to the opposing team for a foul, such as pushing, tripping, or touching the ball with the hands.

2. If the ball goes out of bounds it is kicked back in from the side line by a member of the opposing team.

3. Eliminate players for five minutes for any unnecessary roughness.

Variation

To develop more kicking skill, use goal posts and assign four players as goalkeepers. These four players may catch the ball and throw it out of their area.

20. *One Less*

Equipment: A collection of objects.

Formation

The players line up behind the starting line. About fifteen feet away, on the finish line are the objects to be picked up. These may be Indian clubs, bean bags, blocks of wood, balls, erasers, etc. The number of objects should be one less than the number of players.

Action

On a signal, all the players run forward and attempt to grab one article. Each time one player will be left without an article and this player drops out of the game. Remove one or more articles and have the players run again. Continue until all are eliminated except two players and one article. The winner is the player who retrieves the last article.

Variations

1. Remove several articles at one time. This will make the game move faster.

2. Put the articles in a pile. If there are many players, use several piles.

21. *Poison Pin*

Equipment: Three Indian clubs.

FORMATION

Two equal teams stand, facing each other, in two parallel lines, about twelve feet apart. In the center, there are three Indian clubs, placed in triangular formation, about one foot apart. The players are numbered consecutively from left to right.

ACTION

The first and second players from each team come forward and join hands around the clubs. On a signal, these players try to throw their opponents off balance, thus forcing them to knock over one or more of the clubs. At the same time, they try to avoid knocking over the clubs themselves. As soon as a pin falls, one point is scored against the team that knocked it down. The four players now return to the right of their lines and the third and fourth players from each team come to the center. At the end of the game, the line having the least points is the winner.

VARIATION

The winning couple may defend the clubs until they are defeated.

22. *Punt Ball*

Equipment: One ball, four bases.

FORMATION

The field is marked in the same manner as for softball. There are two teams, one "up" and one in the field. The team in the field has one player on each base including home, while the remaining players are scattered in the field. There is no pitcher.

ACTION

The player "up" may pass, punt, or place-kick the ball. He then runs the bases as in softball. The field players receive the ball and forward-pass it to the basemen to put the runner out or to keep him from advancing bases. The game continues as in softball, with each run counting one point. After three outs, the teams change places.

VARIATIONS

To add interest, designate the type of pass the player "up" shall make, such as: throwing the ball between his legs, throwing it with his back to the field or throwing the ball with his left hand.

To develop greater throwing skill, a player may be called out if the pass from home plate is caught before it touches the ground.

23. Roley-Hop

Equipment: One small ball.

FORMATION

Informal group.

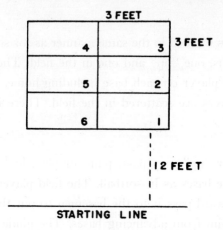

ACTION

From the starting line, the ball is rolled into square 1 and retrieved while in the square. A player bounces the ball once hopping once in each of the six squares. If he accomplishes this without stepping on any line, he is now ready to go on to square 2. This time, the ball is bounced twice and the player hops twice in each square. In rolling the ball into the higher numbers, the player must run through each of the preceding squares before retrieving the ball. This can also be continued by playing the squares in reverse. The player who finishes first wins.

24. *Standing Broad Jump*

Equipment: Jumping area,* a tape measure is optional.

FORMATION

Teach the skill in groups. Then have individuals compete. Players should stand on both feet toeing a line.

* If possible, it is best to dig up an area of ground about 4 feet by 20 feet for the participants to jump on.

Action

Rise on the toes, take a half-deep knee bend, then jump into the air and land on the toes, your body slightly forward. Repeat this skill, jumping forward and increasing the distance. After this skill is learned add the arm action. As you rise on the toes, swing the arms forward and upward. When you bend your knees, the arms should swing downward and backward. Then, jump forward and swing the arms forward and upward again. The body should fall forward as the measurement is taken from the starting line to the nearest point where the body touches the ground.

25. *Squeeze Out*

Formation

A double circle is formed, with partners facing each other. There are two extra players, one the Chaser, the other the Runner.

Action

The Chaser and Runner run around or through the circle. The Runner is safe if he stops between the members of a couple. When the Runner stops, he stands with his back to one of the players. This player is "squeezed out," and he becomes the Chaser, while the former Chaser becomes the Runner. If the Runner is caught, the Chaser becomes the Runner and the Runner the Chaser. Encourage the players to keep the game moving by not running too long, and to make surprise stops between the couples.

26. *Three Shots*

Equipment: A wastebasket or box and one ball for each team.

FORMATION

Equal teams stand behind a throwing line. One wastebasket or box is placed fifteen feet in front of each team. A player stands behind each basket to return the ball and to keep score.

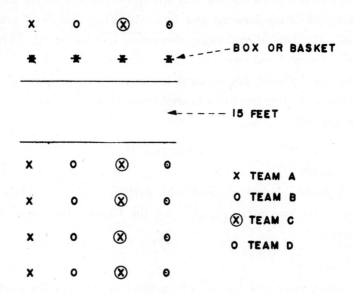

ACTION

The first player on each team has three consecutive shots at the basket. Any type of shot may be used but an underhand toss is suggested. If the ball lands in the basket, one point is scored. When all have had a turn, the team having the most points wins.

27. *Touch Football Tag*

Equipment: One ball.*

*Boys will enjoy using a football if available.

FORMATION

Players are scattered about the playing area. One player has a ball while another is "It."

ACTION

"It" tries to tag the player with the ball. If he succeeds, that player becomes "It." However, the player with the ball may pass the ball to another player and then "It" tries to tag that player. The player with the ball is always the one who is chased. Try to encourage passing the ball as often as possible.

28. *Triangle Run*

FORMATION

A large triangle is marked off with a base at each corner. There are three equal teams, one behind each base.

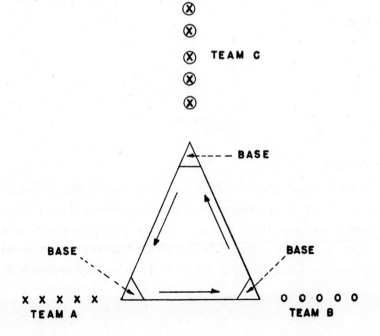

ACTION

On a signal, the first player of each team leaves his base and runs to his right around the triangle, touching each base on the way. When he returns to his base the next player in line does the same. The runners may pass each other, but they must touch each base as they run. The first team back in its original place wins.

29. *Twenty-Five Yard Dash*

Equipment: A stop watch or a watch with a second hand. A straight and level area for running.

FORMATION

One or two players are on a starting line. Mark off a finish line.

ON YOUR   GET SET   GO
MARK

ACTION

On a signal, the contestant runs in a straight line as fast as possible to the finish line. For practice, two or three players run at the same time. When timing the players one runs at a time. The players should be encouraged to run at top speed across the finish line and not slow down as they approach it.

30. *Wide Awake*

Equipment: One ball.

FORMATION

All players stand in a circle, facing the center.

ACTION

The ball is thrown from player to player, but not in any particular order. Any player missing a fair throw is eliminated. An unfair throw is one that is too far overhead, or one too short to be caught. The object is to see who can remain in the game the longest.

VARIATION

Alternate the players, "Reds" and "Blues." At the end of the playing time count how many are left in the circle. The team with the greater number left, wins. The passes should be made to all, not just to opposing players.

RELAYS

31. *Bowling Relay*

Teams are in single lines behind a starting line. One player stands in stride position about twenty feet in front of each team and three feet from a wall. The first player in each line has a ball and attempts to roll it between the opposite player's legs. If he succeeds, the ball goes to the next player in line. If he fails, he takes another turn. Whether this is made or missed, the ball goes to the next player in line. The player opposite each line must not touch the ball until after it goes through his legs or it is definitely missed. In either case, he quickly recovers the ball and rolls it back to his team, returning to his stride position immediately. The team finishing first wins.

The game may also be played for points. Each player has one turn and scores a point each time he successfully rolls the ball between the other player's legs. The team with the highest score wins.

32. *Couple Slide Relay*

An even number of players on each team are in single lines behind a starting line. Each team pairs off in couples. The first couple in each line joins both hands, slides up to a turning line, and returns to place, touching off the next couple. For variation the players may drop their hands at the turning line, swing once around, then slide back to place.

33. *Handy Feet Relay*

Teams are in single lines behind a starting line. About twenty feet from the starting line, place an Indian club and a chair for each team. The first player in each line runs forward and knocks down the Indian club with his feet. Then he sits on the chair and sets up the club using only his feet. When the club is upright, he runs back to place. The next player repeats the process.

34. *Hobble Race Relay*

The teams are in single lines behind a starting line. The first player in each line stands on his left foot, bends his right knee to his chest, and holds his right toe with his left hand. In this position, he hops forward to the turning line, reverses his position and hops back on his other foot, touching off the next player. For variation, have the player hold his toe by the thumb and forefinger. If he releases his foot he must return to the starting line and begin again.

35. *Human Croquet Relay*

Two equal teams line up on a starting line at opposite ends of the playing area. Nine players are chosen to be wickets and stand in stride position as shown in the diagram. On a starting signal, the first player of each team crawls through the first double wicket, the wicket on his right, the center wicket, the next one on his right, and the double wicket at the opposite end, touching the starting line at the opposite end from where he returns to his original place, keeping right. He touches off the next player who follows the same course. If the group is mixed, have the boys play one game and the girls another.

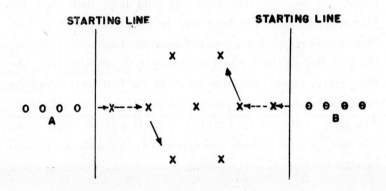

36. *Jump the Ditch Relay*

Teams are in single lines behind a starting line. A good running distance from the starting line, mark off a "Ditch" one yard wide. About twenty feet beyond this, mark off a turning line. The first player in each line runs forward, jumps over the Ditch, runs to the turning line, jumps over the Ditch again on the way back, and returns to place touching off the next player. If a player lands in the Ditch either time, he must go back to the starting line and start again.

37. *Obstacle Hop Relay*

Teams are in single lines behind a starting line. Four eight-inch squares are marked off with chalk on the floor, about two feet apart, in front of each team. These squares represent the "Obstacles." On a line beyond the last Obstacle, there is a bean bag. The first player in each line stands on his right foot and holds his left foot with his left hand. On a signal, each player hops forward to obtain the bean bag, hopping over each Obstacle. He picks up the bean bag and hops back over the Obstacles, handing the bean bag to the next player in line. The second player hops forward over the Obstacles, replacing the bean bag on the line and returning to the starting line. The third player repeats the steps taken by the first player, and the fourth player repeats the process followed by the second player. The game continues until all have run. If a player steps on an Obstacle, he must go back and hop over the Obstacle again until he clears it.

38. *One-Hand Pass Relay*

Players in each team stand a few feet apart in single lines behind a starting line. The first player in each line holds a ball in his right hand. On a signal, he passes the ball back to the next player who receives it in his right hand. This continues all the way down the line. When the last player receives the ball, he runs forward, still holding the ball in his right hand, to a turning line about twenty feet in front of his team, finally returning to the front of his line. The ball is passed back again and the game continues until each one is back in his own place. If a player drops the ball he must recover it, return to his place, and start over.

39. *Quartet Relay*

Each team divides into groups of fours, the players standing side by side with hands joined, behind a starting line. The first "quartet" in each team runs forward to a turning line and, without dropping hands, runs back to touch off the next "quartet." This continues until all groups in each team have run. For variation, have the "quartets" link arms or clasp hands in the back.

40. *Soccer Kick Relay*

Teams are in single lines behind a starting line. A "Kicking" line is drawn about thirty feet from the starting line and parallel to it. The first player in each line dribbles a ball to the Kicking line, stops it, turns around, and kicks it back to the next player in line who repeats the procedure. The players who have had their turn line up behind the Kicking line. The last player in each line dribbles the ball to the Kicking line and holds his hand up to indicate that his team is finished. A team is disqualified if any player uses his hands on the ball.

41. *Steady Hand Relay*

Teams are in single lines behind a starting line. The first player in each team has two pennies. He places the pennies on any two fingers (palms up), extending his arm. On a signal, he runs forward to the turning line and back trying not to drop the pennies. If he drops a penny, he must replace it and continue the race.

42. *Swing Your Partner Relay*

Each team divides into two equal groups, standing fifteen feet apart in a single line, facing each other. The first player in each line skips forward, meets the opposite player on his team, swings him once around and skips back to place, touching off the next player. The team whose line first gets back to its original position wins.

This is an excellent opportunity to teach the correct "Buzz" step in square dancing. The game may also be played hooking right elbows and again hooking left elbows.

DANCES

43. *Arkansas Traveler*
(American)

Record:
Victor 20638

Basic Steps

Sashay; allemande; grand right and left.

Formation

Squares of eight are formed, lady on the gent's right.

Dance

Counts

8   The head lady and the opposite gent walk four steps forward and four steps back.

8   The same dancers walk eight steps forward and change places.

8   The two ladies face, join both hands, and sashay to the opposite side. While they do this, the two gents are sashaying singly to the opposite side allowing the ladies to pass between them. Repeat and return to own place.

8   They repeat the third figure, but this time the gents pass inside.

8   The first and third couples take four steps forward and four steps back.

8   The first and third couples take four steps forward again, and, taking four counts swing their partner back to place.

32   All do allemande left, then a grand right and left. They meet the partner at home and swing her once around. Repeat all with the second lady and fourth gent leading off.

44. *Army and Navy Dance*
(American)

Record:

Victor 20191

(El Capitan March)

BASIC STEPS

March; hop; skip; polka.

FORMATION

Double lines are formed, partners opposite each other, all facing front.

DANCE

Part 1. The Army

Figure 1. Marching

Counts

16   Take six marching steps forward, face your partner, and salute on counts seven and eight. Turn and march six steps back to place, face your partner, and salute.

Figure 2. The Square

16   March three steps forward, passing left shoulders, changing places. Turn left, and again march three steps forward. After doing this twice more a square is completed. Repeat figure 2.

Figure 3. Sliding

16   Put your hands on the hips, facing partner. Take four slides toward the front of the room, followed by four marking-time steps in place. Slide back again, eight counts. Repeat, omitting the last four marking-time steps (twelve counts) and march up to the partner on the last four counts. Stand shoulder to shoulder, facing left.

Figure 4. Wheeling

16   Take four steps (half circle) into your partner's place. On counts five and six, step away from your partner. On counts seven and eight, step toward your partner (side step). Take four steps (half circle) into your own place. Take four backward steps to the original position.

Figure 5. Sliding

16   Put your hands on the hips. Slide four steps toward the front of the room, then mark time four counts. Slide back four steps to place, then mark time four counts. Salute.

Part 2. The Navy

FORMATION

All are facing front.

Figure 1. Sail Hoisting

16   Right arm raised, pull down right, bending your knees, then straighten the knees and rise. This action takes two counts. Left arm raised high, pull down with the left arm, bending your knees. Repeat the above three times and on the last two counts, do not bend the knees.

Figure 2. Looking out to Sea

16   Shade your eyes with the right hand, take four hops on the right foot, extending the left leg backward. Change hands and repeat the hops left. Repeat the hops right and left.

Figure 3

16   Repeat figure 1.

Figure 4

16   Repeat figure 2.

Figure 5. The "Hornpipe"

32   Fold arms high on the chest. Take eight backward skips, starting with the left foot, then do four polka steps forward, starting with the left foot. Repeat eight backward skips, starting with the left foot, then three polka steps forward, starting with the left foot. Face your partner and salute.

45. *Bavarian Dance*

BASIC STEPS

Step swing; hop waltz.

FORMATION

Dancers form double circle, girl on the outside. The inside hands are joined, the outside hands being on the hips.

DANCE

Both start with the outside foot.

Part 1

Measures

1-4   Take four step swings, and face your partner.

5-8   Take four waltz steps, making one complete turn to the right. Hands are joined, arms extended out to the sides. The boy starts with the left foot and the girl with the right.

9-16   Repeat all.

Part 2

Partners face, arms akimbo.

17-18   Take two step swings, moving backward, boy left, girl right, boy right, girl left.

19   Take three running steps backward. This has brought all the boys together in the center of the circle. The girls have moved outward.

20   The boys turn right to the center, bring their feet together on count 1, they bow on counts 2, 3. At the same time, the girls, with their backs to the boys, bow on counts 1, 2, 3.

21-24   Repeat part 2, this time moving toward each other and bowing to each other.

25-28   Take four step swings.

29-32   Take four hop-waltz steps.

46. *Cracoviac*
(Poland)

Record:
Folkraft: F1102

BASIC STEPS

Balance; polka.

FORMATION

Dancers form double circle, girl on the outside.

DANCE

Figure 1

Measures

1-4 Take four balance steps forward and backward. Inside hands are joined and arms swing forward and backward.

5 Walk two steps forward, beginning with the outside foot.

6 Stamp three times.

7-8 Repeat measures 5 and 6.

Figure 2

9-16 In social dance position, polka eight steps around the circle.

17-32 Repeat all.

47. *Military Two-Step*

Record:
Decca 2091A

BASIC STEPS

Walk; two-step.

FORMATION

Double circle is formed, facing the line of direction. Girl takes boy's arm.

DANCE

Starting with the outside foot, walk forward eight steps. Drop the arms and face your partner. Partners separate by walking four steps backward, then bow. Walk four steps back to your partner and take social dance position. Dance eight two-steps.

48. *Money Musk*
(American)

Record:
Victor: 20447A

BASIC STEPS

Cast-off; right and left through.

FORMATION

Six couples in two parallel lines. The fourth and the first couples can dance at the same time. Directions are given for the first couple.

DANCE

Counts

8   The first couple joins both hands and circles one and a half times around, to finish standing between the second and third couples.

8   These six dancers join hands and move four steps forward, then four steps back to place.

8   The first couple again turns in the center three-quarters of a turn to finish sideways, the girl between the third couple and the boy between the second couple.

8   These six dancers join hands and move forward four steps, then four steps back to place.

8   "Cast-off," the second couple. The first couple turns three-quarters of a turn and finishes between the second and third couples.

8   The first and second couples take a right and left through and back. The dance is repeated from the beginning. After the first couple has "cast-off" three couples, the second couple becomes the head couple.

49. *Multiplication Dance*

BASIC STEP

Waltz.

FORMATION

The girls line up on one side of the room and the boys on the other. One couple is chosen to go to the center and start the dance.

DANCE

The couple in the center starts to waltz when the music begins. When the music stops, this couple separates. The girl chooses a new partner from the boys' line and the boy chooses one from the girls' line. These couples waltz, then stop and choose new partners as before. Thus the dancers multiply until all are dancing.

VARIATIONS

Many dance steps can be used: Polka; Foxtrot; Two-Step; Varsouvianna; Gavotte.

50. *New Century Hornpipe*
(Irish)

Record:
Victor 20592A
(Soldiers Joy)

BASIC STEPS

Balance; swing, ladies' chain; right and left.

FORMATION

Six couples in two parallel lines, partners facing.

DANCE

Counts

4   The first couple balances at the head.

12   The first couple joins both hands and swings one and a half times around to the opposite place.

16   The first and second couples do ladies' chain.

4   The first couple balances in the center.

12   The first couple swings again one and a half times around, finishing the swing one place below the second couple. This "casts-off" the second couple. They are now at the head of the set.

16   The second and first couples do right and left through and right and left back.

The figures are repeated by the first couple each time they "cast-off" another couple. After three couples have been "cast-off," the new head couple also starts the figure, and the dance continues.

51. *Norwegian Mountain March*
(Norwegian)

Record:
Victor 20151

BASIC STEPS

Run; step-hop.

FORMATION

Two girls stand close behind one boy. The two girls join inside hands and the boy reaches back and takes each girl's free hand.

DANCE

Part 1

Measures   Counts*

1-2   6   Starting with the right foot, all run forward three steps and bend their bodies to the right. They repeat this with the left foot and bend left.

* When record is used.

3-8   15   They continue five more times, end-
ing with their feet together.

Repeat

1-8

Part 2

Without letting go of hands all do a step-hop in place until it
is their turn to move:

Measures   Counts

9-12   6   1. The boy moves backward with six
step-hops, under the girls' raised arms.

13-16   6   2. The girl on his left takes six step-
hops to cross and goes under the boy's raised right arm.

9-12   6   3. The other girl takes six step-hops
turning under the boy's raised right arm.

13-16   4   4. The boy turns under his right arm
with four step-hops.

Repeat from the beginning.

52. *O'Susie*
(American)

Record:

Victor 20638A

(Quadrille Figure 3)

BASIC STEPS

Slide; make a basket; swing the lady; promenade.

FORMATION

Partners are in a single circle, lady on the gent's right.

Dance

Part 1

Counts

8	Take eight slides, circling to the right.
8	Take eight slides circling to the left.
4	Walk four steps to the center.
4	Walk four steps back to your place.
8	Swing your partners and all face the center.

Part 2

4   Ladies take four steps to the center, gents clap hands.

4   Ladies walk back to their place, gents clap hands.

4   Gents take four steps to the center, ladies clap hands.

4   Gents walk back to their place, ladies clap hands.

8   Clap hands eight times, give the right hand to your partner and turn once around to your place.

8   Clap hands eight times, give the left hand to your neighbor and turn once around to your place, then face center.

Part 3

4   Ladies walk to the center and stay there.

4   All clap hands four times.

4   Gents walk to the center, keeping their partner on their right.

4   All clap hands four times.

8   Make a basket.

8   The basket circles eight steps to the right.

8   The basket circles eight steps to the left.

Part 4

8   Break the basket.

4   All take four steps backward to their place.

8   Couples, in promenade position, take four steps to the center then four steps back to their place. On the last four counts, they face the line of direction.

16   All promenade around the circle. Repeat all. Finish with bow to your partner.

53. Oxford Minuet

Records:

Decca 2091B

Decca 25059

Basic Steps

Walk; toe point; two-step.

Formation

Dancers stand in double circle, partners facing, holding hands at arm's length.

Dance (Directions are given for the gentleman.)

Walk to the right three steps and touch the right heel forward. Repeat the three steps and heel touch to the left. Touch the right toe to the right, bring your feet together, touch the left toe to the left. Repeat twice. Then all dance the two-step.

54. *Pass the Shoe*
(Dutch)

You must pass this shoe from me to you, to you,
You must pass this shoe and do just what I do.

FORMATION

All sit in one large circle. Each player has one of his shoes in his right hand. They sing the song in unison.

DANCE

As they sing the song, each player passes the shoe to the right on beats 1, 2, 3, 4, 5 and 6. On beat 7, the shoe is not passed; it is tapped on the floor to the right. On beat 8, it is tapped to the left. (The shoe is kept in the same hand.) On beat 9, the shoe is again passed to the right. Any player that misses is eliminated, this player and a shoe being taken from the circle.

VARIATIONS

When the group has mastered the coordination and become more expert, its members may play with two shoes. If the group is very large, the players may form more than one circle.

55. *Paul Jones*

Music:

Any good March

This is a good social mixer. It changes partners easily and frequently. The teacher or caller can use any figure she chooses and can call the changes as often as desired.

Basic Steps

March; grand right and left; two-step.

Formation

The gentlemen choose a partner and the couples line up two by two around the room.

Dance

Any or all of the following figures may be used: March around two by two. March by fours. All face center and circle to the right. All walk forward to the center and back to their place. All circle to the left. Face your partner and take grand right and left. When the music stops, take for a new partner the child who holds your right hand. All two-step around the room. The ladies go to the center and make a circle, the gents make their circle around the outside. The ladies circle to the right and the gents to the left. When the music stops, the ladies face the gents and take the gents standing opposite them as new partners. All two-step around the room. On a signal, the gents' line stands still and the ladies' line continues on for ten steps. The new partners two-step around the room. This can be repeated, with the ladies standing still and the gents moving on. All two-step.

56. *Push the Business On*

I'll buy a horse and steal a gig,
And all the world will dance a jig,
And I'll do all that ever I can
To push the business on,
To push the business on.
And I'll do all that ever I can
To push the business on.

BASIC STEP

Slide.

FORMATION

Single circle is formed, hands joined, the ladies on the right.

DANCE

Measures

1-4   The circle moves to the right with eight slides.

5-6   Drop the hands and place them on your hips.
Turn in place to the right; end the turn facing your partner.

7-8   Clap 1, 2, 3, raising your hands at the third clap.
Clap high.

9-10   Repeat claps.

11-12   Partners join both hands and turn once around
to the right and back to place. The lady ends this turn standing
directly in front of her gent.

13-14   The gents place both hands at their ladies' waists
and "hops" her to the right, to a new gent, who receives his new
lady from the left.

57. *Rheinlander*
(Swedish)

BASIC STEPS

Schottische; step-hop.

FORMATION

Double circle is formed facing the line of direction.

DANCE

1-4   Starting with the outside foot, run slightly away from your partner three steps and hop, swinging the free foot forward. Repeat these steps, running toward your partner.

5-8   Face your partner and take four step-hops, turning in place. The girl puts both hands on the boy's shoulder, who places his hands at her waist. Repeat all.

58. *Shoo Fly*
(American Civil War Period)

Record:

Folkraft F1102

Shoo fly, don't bother me,
Shoo fly, don't bother me,
Shoo fly, don't bother me,
For I belong to somebody.

Chorus: I feel, I feel, I feel, I feel like a morning star.
I feel, I feel, I feel, I feel like a morning star.

BASIC STEP

Walk; swing the lady.

FORMATION

Single circle is formed, hands joined, the lady on the gent's right.

DANCE

Measures

1-2   Take four steps to the center, raising your hands forward and up.

3-4   Take four steps back to place, lowering the hands.

5-8   Repeat.

9-15   Join both hands and partners turn around in place. On count 15, stop the swing with the lady on the gent's left. The lady turns under the raised left hands.

16   This will give each gent a new lady on his right. Repeat all.

VARIATION

Turn the circle inside out.

DANCE

The circle moves four steps in and four steps out, then repeats. The hands remain joined for the next sixteen measures. One couple is assigned to make the arch; they raise their joined hands. The couple directly opposite walks forward, everyone following, hands still joined, and they walk under the arch. When all the couples have gone under the arch, the couple that formed the arch, turns under the arched hands, and the circle has turned inside out.

The dance may now be repeated, working backward. This time, when the gent puts the lady on his other side, they all face center again and are ready to dance as in the first part.

59. *Skip to My Lou*

Record:
Folkraft F1103

Flies in the buttermilk, two by two,
Flies in the buttermilk, shoo, fly, shoo.
Flies in the buttermilk, two by two,
Skip to my Lou, my darlin'.

Basic Step

Skip.

Formation

Single circle of partners is formed with the lady on the gent's right. One couple stands in the middle of the circle.

Dance

As the group sings the song, the center couple skips around the circle. They stop in front of one of the circle players and he joins hands with them. Then all three dancers skip around. As they sing the last line, the original couple raises the joined hands and the third player skips under the arch they have formed. The couple now joins the circle and the dancer left calls in another couple as before and on the word "skip" the odd player goes under the arch and on to choose a new couple as the old couple joins the circle. This continues as long as desired.

Note

This is a simple action, but will help to teach the children timing, and to change places quickly.

60. *Southern Schottische*

Record:

Henry Ford 103B

Basic Steps

Walk; slow schottische.

Formation

Double circle is formed, facing the line of direction, girl on the outside.

Dance

Counts

16   The backs of the hands are on the hips. Starting on the left foot, walk forward seven steps. On count 8, face and bow to your partner. Return to your place with seven walking steps and bow.

16   Take one slow schottische step to your own right, then left, right, left.

16   Take one slow schottische step to your own right, clap hands 1, 2, 3, 4. Repeat to the left.

16   Take one slow schottische step to your own right, stamp left, right, left, right. Repeat to the left.

16   Partners
are facing, right
hands held high.

Take four schottische
steps, circling each
other around to your
own place. Repeat,
your left hands held high. Partners face the line of direction,
inside hands joined and take schottische forward. Repeat all.

61. *Swedish Varsouvianna*

BASIC STEPS

Step; swing; waltz.

FORMATION

The gentleman stands slightly behind his lady. They both hold their arms to the side, hands joined, shoulder high.

DANCE

Part 1

Measures

1   Take three walking steps forward right, left, right.

2   Turn your bodies slightly to the left and point the left toe; hold two counts.

3   Repeat measure 1 starting with the left foot and moving to the left.

4   Turn right; point the right toe; hold.

5-8   Repeat measures 1-4.

Part 2

9   Beginning right, walk two steps forward, then swing your right foot forward (1), then the left foot (2), hop on the left foot, at the same time swinging the right foot forward (3).

10   Repeat measure 9.

11-12   Repeat measures 1-2 to the right.

13-16   Repeat measures 9-12 to the left; finish with partners facing.

Part 3

9-16   In social dance position, waltz and repeat measures 9-16. On the last measure, the gentleman stamps twice as the lady returns to the original position.

62. *The Black Nag*

(English)

Record:

Victor 20444

BASIC STEPS

A double; slip step; turn single; partner's arm; whole-hey.

FORMATION

Sets of six are standing longways.

DANCE

Part 1

Measures

1-4   All walk up a double and back to place a double.

5-8   Repeat.

1-2   The first boy and first girl face each other and take four slip steps down to the foot of the set.

3-4   The second couple does the same.

5-6   The third couple does the same.

7-8   All turn single.

1-2   The third couple takes four slip steps back to place.

3-4   The second couple does the same.

5-6   The first couple does the same.

7-8   All turn single.

Part 2

1-4   Partners slide. Join hands and slide once around to place.

5-8   Repeat.

1-2   The first boy and the third girl change places with slip steps.

3-4   The first girl changes places with the third boy.

5-6   The second boy and second girl change places.

7-8   All turn single.

1-8   Repeat part 2.

Part 3

1-4   Partners hook right elbows and turn once around.

5-8   Partners hook left elbows and turn once around.

1-8   The boys whole-hey on their own side.

1-8   The girls whole-hey on their own side. Repeat the dance from the beginning.

63. *The Circle with Six*
(American)

Record:
Victor 22991
(Sicilian Circle)

BASIC STEPS

Slide; ladies chain; forward and pass through.

FORMATION

Circles of six people are formed. If possible, the gents stand in the middle of the three and a lady on each side.

DANCE

Circle six hands around. Gents swing the opposite lady on the right. Right-hand ladies chain. Left-hand ladies chain. Circle three hands around, to the left, then to the right. Threes take four steps forward and four steps back. Threes walk forward again and this time pass through to meet the next group. They all pass right shoulders.

64. *The Hesitation Waltz*

Music:
Any good waltz

Basic Step

Hesitation step; moving forward and backward.

Formation

Dancers take social dance position.

Dance

It will be best to have the dancers practise the step alone until they can progress smoothly and easily.

Counts

Start with your feet together.

1	Step forward on the left foot.
2	Swing the right leg forward and past the left foot.
3	Touch the right toe lightly forward.
1	Step backward on the right foot.
2	Swing the left leg backward and past the right foot.
3	Touch the left toe lightly forward.

The regular waltz may be followed by one of these balances, or the balance may be continued for several measures. The dancers may also turn as they balance, if they like.

65. *The Rye Waltz*

Records:
Ford 107B
Folkraft 1044

Basic Steps

Toe point; slide; waltz.

FORMATION

Dancers are in social dance position. Directions are given for the boy.

DANCE

Point your left toe forward, point your left toe close to the right heel. Repeat. Take three slides and hold one count. Without changing the arm position, repeat both steps in the opposite direction. Repeat again left and then right (thirty-two counts). Take twelve waltz steps. Partners step back from each other and bow. Repeat all.

66. *The Shamrock*
(Irish)

Records:
Victor 21616A
Decca 3000A

BASIC STEPS

Step-swing; elbow swing.

FORMATION

Double circle is formed, partners facing, girl on the outside.

DANCE

Counts

2   Step and stamp to the right and swing the left foot across and in front of the right. Both hands are on the hips.

6   Repeat to the left, right, and left.

8   Take four step-hops backward  away from your partner; then take four step-hops back to place. Start on the right foot.

8   Repeat the four step swings, beginning right.

8   Hook right elbows with your partner and take four step-hops around to place. Repeat hooking left elbows. Move to the right to meet a new partner on the last step-hop.

67. *The Wild Irishman*

(American)

Record:

Victor 21616

(Irish Washerwoman)

BASIC STEPS

Swing the lady; allemande; grand right and left; sashay.

FORMATION

Squares of eight are formed, one extra dancer being in the center of each square.

DANCE

Counts

8	The extra dancer swings the lady of the first couple.
8	Then he swings the lady of the third couple.
8	All allemande left, the extra dancer clapping hands.

16 Take grand right and left.

8 The extra dancer swings the lady of the second couple.

8 Then he swings the lady of the fourth couple.

8 All allemande left.

16 Take grand right and left. As this is being danced, the extra dancer, "the wild Irishman," attempts to cut in the chain to steal a lady. The gent, cut out, goes to the center.

16 Promenade.

68. *Waltz Quadrille*
(American)

Record:
Any good waltz.

BASIC STEP

Waltz.

FORMATION

Squares of eight are formed, lady on the gent's right.

DANCE

Counts

4 Honor Corners.

4 Honor Partners.

8 Couples No. 1 and No. 3 waltz forward and back.

8 Couples No. 1 and No. 3 waltz with their partners once around the set.

8 The gents No. 1 and No. 3, waltz their corner lady once around the set.

32 Couples No. 2 and No. 4 repeat the figures.

8   The four ladies waltz to the center, join hands and waltz half way around, finishing beside the opposite gent.

8   Gents do the same and waltz to their partner.

8   Ladies waltz to their own places.

8   Gents return.

32   All waltz around the set.

16   Waltz the grand chain.

16   Couple No. 1 waltz around the outside of the set.

48   Couples No. 2, No. 3, No. 4 the same in succession.

16   Couples No. 1 and No. 3 change partners and waltz.

16   Couples No. 2 and No. 4 the same. Waltz as long as they wish.

69. *Weaving Cloth*
(Swedish)

Record:
Victor 21616B Part 2
(Irish Washerwoman)

BASIC STEPS

Easy running step, reel, shuffle.

FORMATION

About five couples in a longways set.

DANCE

Figure 1

The top couple join inside hands and run eight steps to the foot of the set, change hands and run eight steps back to place.

Figure 2

The top couple reels to the foot of the set. The gent reels the ladies, the lady the gents.

Figure 3

The weaving step: The top couple has reached the foot of the set. All couples place hands on their partners' shoulders, this makes the loom. They all use a shuffle step and push each other backward and forward with three shuffle steps. Couples No. 2 and No. 4 move forward at the same time couples No. 3 and No. 5 move backward. The top couple is the shuttle and they, with the same shuffle step, weave backward then forward in and out the other dancers to the top of the set.

Figure 4

All, except the top couple, kneel on the right knee and clap hands. The top couple join inside hands and carrying the hands over the heads of those of the right side line, run to the foot of the set, then continue down the left side of the set.

Figure 5 (If record is used)

All give right hands to partners and turn once around eight steps, join left hands and turn once around eight steps.

Figure 6

All dancers join hands to make an archway, the top couple runs eight steps under the archway to the foot of the set.

SELF-TESTING ACTIVITIES

70. *Balance Bend*

Stand with your heels against a wall. Bend from the waist, keeping the heels on the floor, and pick up a small object such as a piece of chalk or a penny that is placed about two inches from the toe of the right foot.

71. *Back to Back Pull Over*

Two players stand back to back and hook elbows. The second player bends forward and the first player leans backward resting on the second player's back. The second player exerts a strong pull with his arms and, at the same time, the first player springs from the floor and rolls over the back of the second player, landing on his feet, facing his partner. Partners should be about the same size.

72. *Caterpillar Walk*

The first player places his hands and knees on the floor. The second player sits in a stride position on the shoulders of the first player and leans forward, placing his hands on the floor in front of the first player. In this position, they proceed forward, both moving their right hands and then their left hands. The second player should not touch the floor with his feet. This may be done with several couples in a line.

73. *Couple Bear Dance*

Take a squat position, facing a partner and join hands. Extend the right leg forward. With a quick change of weight, draw the extended leg back and place the other leg forward. Repeat this change in rapid succession. After doing it in place, try moving in one direction for a designated distance. Couples may compete against each other.

74. *Elbow Dip*

Take a squat position on the floor and extend the legs back. The body should be straight. Bend the elbows and pick up a piece of paper from the floor with the teeth. The paper is folded so that the top is three or four inches from the floor and it is placed directly under the face.

75. *Flying Angel*

The first player lies on his back on a mat and bends his knees to his chest with the feet parallel to the floor, extending both

arms upward. The second player places the feet of the first player
on the front part of his hips, leans forward,
clasps the hands of the first player and
straightens his legs, pushing the second
player up so that his body is straight and
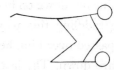
parallel to the floor. This position is held for a few seconds.

76. *Merry-Go-Round*

Eight people stand in a circle facing the center. Every other
person lies down on the floor on his back with the legs toward
the center, all feet touching. Each player who is standing reaches
down and clasps hands with the person on each side of him
raising him about a foot from the floor and walking around in
a circle to the right. Each player in the reclining position should
arch his back, keep his body rigid, and use his feet as a pivot.
Have several groups do this at the same time and note which
one can turn the longest without breaking hold.

77. *Siamese Hop*

Players stand back to back with their weight on the right foot.
Each grasps the ankle of a partner's free foot and hops a designated distance in one direction. Couples may compete against
each other for distance or speed.

78. *Skin the Snake*

Several players stand in a stride position in a single file. Each
player reaches his right hand back between his legs and grasps

the left hand of the player behind him. The last player in the line lies down on his back as the rest of the line moves backward, straddling this player. When the next to the last player has passed over him, he lies down as does each one in turn until all are down. The last player to lie down gets up and walks forward and pulls each one up in succession to the starting position. The hands must be clasped throughout the whole procedure. Groups may compete against each other to see who can get back in position first. If the class is mixed, have the girls form one line and the boys another.

79. *Spinning Wheel*

Take a squat position and place your hands on the floor on each side. Extend the left leg forward and swing the left leg to the right and under the right hand. Hop on the right foot and pass the left leg under the right foot. Continue circling the left leg, passing under the left hand and back to place. Repeat, doing it slowly at first and then increase the speed until the movement is continuous. Try and keep the extended leg straight. This may also be done with the right leg forward making a circle to the left.

80. *Stick Twist*

Hold a stick or wand in front of your body with both hands, palms down. Cross your arms with palms up, keeping a firm grasp on the stick. Place your head through the opening made by your crossed arms and the stick. Work the stick down over the shoulders and back without releasing the grasp. When the stick is near the floor, step back over the stick one foot at a time. Retain the grasp on the stick, step back into the opening between the crossed arms and the stick and reverse the procedure.

81. *Thigh Balance*

Two players stand side by side, about four feet apart. Each extends the inside foot to the side with the knee bent. A third player places one foot on the thigh of each player and balances himself in a standing position between the two players with his arms extended to the side,  shoulder high. The two players forming the base place their inside hands on the top player's hips.

82. *Tight-Rope Walk*

Draw a chalk mark on the floor, about thirty feet long. Take a squat position at one end and place your hands behind the neck with the elbows back. Travel along the line in this position without losing your balance. Other stunts may be substituted, such as walking on a line, balancing a book or ruler on the head, or balancing a ruler on one finger, without dropping the object.

83. *Toe Lift*

Place a small ball or other object on the toe of one foot. Raise the foot forward, tossing the object in the air and catch it with both hands. Repeat catching the object with one hand.

84. *Triple Rolls*

Three players lie, face down, on a mat about three feet apart. The first player is in the center with the second player on his right and the third player on his left. The first player starts the stunt by rolling to his right. The second player jumps up, leaps over the first player and rolls to his left. The third player jumps up, leaps over the second player and rolls to his right. The third player is now in the center. The stunt continues with the third player rolling to his right and the second player leaping and rolling to the center. The players are constantly in motion.

85. *Wooden Man*

One player lies on his back on a mat with arms close to his side and his body rigid. Two other players take him by the shoulders and lift him to a standing position.

86. *Wall Hop*

Place the weight on one foot and place the other foot against a wall. Hop over this foot without removing it from the wall.

87. *Bull-Dog Pull*

Two players stand facing each other and clasping right hands. Each tries to pull the other over his own goal line that is ten feet behind him.

88. *Champion of the Ring*

Several circles are drawn on the floor, about six feet in diameter. One player stands in each circle and challenges another player. There are now two players in each circle and each stands on the right foot, folding his arms across the chest. Each hops around trying to push the opposing player out of the circle or make him lose his balance. The one who succeeds, wins the bout. He then challenges another player. The player who wins the most bouts in a given length of time is "Champion of the Ring."

89. *Crane Wrestle*

Two players stand facing each other, with the weight on the right foot and clasping right hands. Each player tries to push the other so that he loses his balance and touches the floor with his free foot.

90. *Hand Push*

Two players stand close together, facing each other. Each bends his arms with his hands shoulder high placing them against the opponent's hands. The contestants push with their hands and attempt to force each other to take a step backward.

91. *Head Push*

Stand about two feet from a wall. Place your hands and head against the wall. Remove your hands and fold your arms across the chest. Return to standing position without using your hands. Repeat this several times, increasing the distance from the wall each time.

92. *Kangaroo Fight*

Two players stand in a circle, about six feet in diameter. Each player places a bean bag or folded newspaper between his knees and folds his arms across his chest. Each hops around trying to push the other out of the circle. If a player is forced out of the circle or drops the object between his knees he loses the contest.

93. *Knee Wrestle*

Opponents take kneeling position on a mat about arms' length apart. They grasp right hands and try to push or pull each other off balance.

GLOSSARY

A Double: Two steps forward then two steps backward.

Allemande Left: Gent and corner lady face each other, join left hands, turn once around and return to place.

Allemande Right: Partners face, join right hands, turn once around and finish in original places.

Balance Four: Partners face, join both hands, take seven slide steps to the other end of the set, and without turning, take seven slide steps back to their original places. Couples number one and number three do this as couples number two and number four balance forward together.

Balance Step:

Simple Balance—Point right toe and bring feet together, point left toe and bring feet together.

Western Balance—Partners face, move backward four steps, then forward four steps to place.

American Country Dance Balance—Two steps forward, then two steps backward; or step to side with right foot, close left, and repeat to the left side.

Bending and Twisting: Moving any part of the body out of a straight line.

Bleking Step: (Directions are given for individual dancers.) Jump and place right heel forward. As this is done, the right arm is extended with elbow straight, and the left arm is pulled back with elbow bent. Jump and place the left heel forward and reverse the positions of the arms.

BUZZ STEP: Partners face each other and stand side by side with hips almost touching. The inside feet are used as pivots while pushing with the outside feet.

CAST-OFF: Partners moving away from each other, usually down the outside of the set.

DO-SI-DO: Partners face, then move around each other passing right shoulders, then back to back, then pass left shoulders and move back to own places. Each dancer makes a figure eight.

DOWN THE CENTER AND CUT-OFF FOUR: Couple number one walks down the center and separates in front of couple number three. The lady goes to the right and the gent goes to the left to pass between couples number three and number four, thus cutting off couple number four. This figure is used to cut-off any couple whose number is called.

ELBOW SWING: Partners face, hook right elbows, and make one complete turn, then go on to the next dancer and hook left elbows. The process is repeated, alternating elbows.

FOX TROT: A walking step to two beats of music which consists of stepping forward on the left foot, then on the right. The step is long and the walk is slow.

GALLOPING: Rapid progression by moving forward on one foot, drawing the other foot up quickly, taking the weight on this foot, then stepping forward again. The same foot leads.

GRAND RIGHT AND LEFT: Partners face and join hands, then walk by each other, passing right shoulders. Dropping their hands, they walk forward to meet the next person with whom they join left hands and pass left shoulders. Dropping

their hands, they walk forward to meet the next person
with their right hands. This alternating is continued until
the original place is reached. The dancer always walks
around the circle in the direction in which he started (gents
go counterclockwise and ladies go clockwise).

GRAPEVINE: Step to the side on the left foot, step the right foot
behind the left, step to side on the left foot and step the right
foot in front of the left foot.

HANDS ALL: All hands join in a circle and do a slip or slide step,
as directed.

HALF-HEY: Number one and number three face down and
number two faces up. There are six changes—(a) Number
one and number two pass right shoulders while number
three moves around loop a-b; (b) Number one and number
three pass left shoulders while number two moves around
loop c-d; (c) Number two and number three pass right
shoulders while number one moves around loop a-b. Numbers one and three have changed ends.

Whole-Hey—This is the second half of this figure: (d) Number one and number two pass left shoulders while number
three moves around loop c-d; (e) Number one and number
three pass right shoulders while number two moves around
loop a-b; (f) Number two and number three pass left shoulders while number one moves around loop c-d. This returns
the dancers to their original places.

HEEL AND TOE POLKA: Hop on the left foot, and touch the
right heel forward. Hop on the left foot and touch the right
toe in back.

Polka Forward—Step forward with the right foot, then bring
the feet together. Step forward again on the right foot, and
repeat the step.

Hopping: Moving by a quick springing upward on one foot and landing on the same foot.

Hop Waltz: Partners face, with arms raised sideward at shoulder level and hands joined. The gent step-hops on the right foot and raises his left leg out to the side. The step is repeated with the left foot. The body bends from side to side with each step. The lady does the same step, using the foot opposite to that of her partner.

Jumping: Lifting the body into the air from one or both feet by bending and then extending the knees.

Ladies' Chain: Two couples face each other. The gents stand in place while the ladies walk forward, join right hands and pass each other. They then drop hands and join left hands with those of the gents opposite. Gents place their right hands on the ladies' waists, turn them around in four steps to face the other couple. Repeat, returning to place if the call "ladies' chain back" is given. There are sixteen counts to this step.

Leaping: Covering a distance by pushing off the floor with one foot and landing on the other foot.

Left Hand Star: See Right Hand Star.

Make a Basket: Ladies go to the center and join hands, while the gents join hands around them. Gents move in to the left of their partners, raise joined hands over the ladies' heads and down in front of the ladies. All hands remain joined as the "basket" circles.

Turn the Basket Inside Out—Gents raise their arms back over the ladies' heads. Ladies raise their joined hands over the heads of the gents. Their arms are now across the gents' backs. All hands remain joined as the "basket" circles.

Marching: Walking in regular even steps in a stately manner.

PARTNERS ARM : Partners meet and hook right arms, turn once around and return to place. They then do the same with the left arms.

PARTNERS SIDE : Partners change places, passing right shoulders, and face each other on the opposite sides, returning to places by passing left shoulders.

POLKA FORWARD : See Heel and Toe Polka.

POLKA STEP : Hop on the left foot, step forward on the right foot, bringing the left foot to the right while placing the weight on the right foot. Step forward again on the right foot, etc. Hopping is done on alternate feet for variety.

PROMENADE : Couples move counterclockwise. The gent has his lady on his right and her left hand rests on his right shoulder. He takes her left hand in his and places his right hand at her waist on her right side. A skip, sashay, or polka step may be used as the couples promenade.

REEL : The ladies turn the gents around and the gents turn the ladies around. Partners hook their right elbows and turn once around, then hook their left elbows with the next person in line and turn once around, then return to their partners, hook right elbows and go on to the next person in line.

RIGHT AND LEFT THROUGH : Two couples face and walk toward each other, the gents joining hands with those of the opposite ladies. The couples pass through, ladies to the outside. They drop hands, the partners joining their left hands, as the gents place their right hands at their partners' sides and turn them around in four steps to face the other couple. They repeat and return to places when the call "right and left back" is given. This step is completed in eight counts each way.

RUNNING: A fast walk on the balls of the feet with springing steps.

RIGHT HAND STAR: Four people turn their right sides toward the center of a circle, joining right hands and holding arms high, and then walk clockwise in this formation. The position is reversed for the left hand star. There are eight counts for each direction.

SASHAY: A two-step which can also be done as a slide or glide with the feet close to the floor.

SCHOTTISCHE: Three running steps and a hop done in smooth even rhythm. The free foot often swings forward and crosses the other instead of a hop.

SCOTTISCHE TO THE SIDE: Step sideward to the right on the right foot, and bring the feet together. Step again to the right with the right foot, hop on the right and swing the left foot forward and across the right.

SET: A curtsey in which a step is taken to the right and then the feet are brought together, followed by a step to the left and bringing the feet together. This is done very lightly on the toes, barely taking the weight at the side.

SLIDE POLKA: Two sliding motions followed by three steps, i. e., slide—slide—step—step—step.

SLIDING: A smooth movement, usually done to the side by stepping on one foot, drawing the other foot up and shifting the weight to this foot.

STAMP STEP: A slow strong step, i. e., step right—stamp left; step left—stamp right.

STEP-HOP: Step forward on the right foot and hop on it, then repeat with the left.

STEP-SWING: Stepping on the right foot and swinging the left leg forward, keeping the knee straight and repeating on the left foot.

STRETCHING : Extending the limbs or body.

SWING THE LADY : Partners, facing, stand side by side with hips almost touching, then move around to the right by using the inside feet as pivots while pushing with the outside feet.

THE GRAND SQUARE : Figure in which all the couples move at the same time, each dancer completing a square. The side dancers turn back to back, walk four steps to the corner, make a quarter turn, walk four steps to the head of the set, make a quarter turn, walk four steps to the center to meet new partners, make a quarter turn, and walk four steps back to places. At the same time, the first and third couples walk four steps to the center, meet new partners, make a quarter turn, walk four steps forward, make a quarter turn and walk four steps back to places. The movements are completed in sixteen counts.

TIPTOE : A position of holding or carrying the body weight on the tips of the toes.

TURN THE BASKET INSIDE OUT : See Make a Basket.

TURN SINGLE : Turning with four small running steps as directed.

TWO STEP : *4/4 Fox-Trot Style*—step left, close right, step left, step right, close left, step right, etc. *2/4 Square-Dance Style*-Alternating the two feet in a step—close—hold.

VARSOUVIENNE POSITION : Partners face the line of direction with the lady slightly in front of and to the right of the gentleman. He holds the lady's left hand shoulder high in his own left hand, his right arm extends across the lady's back and he holds her right hand in his right hand.

Walking: Movement from one foot to the other in even rhythm. Body weight is transferred from heel to toe.

Waltz Balance:

Forward—Step forward left, close right, rise on both toes, lower left heel.

Backward—Step back right, close left, rise on toes of both feet, lower right heel.

Sideward—Step sideward left, close right, rise on toes of both feet, lower left heel.

Waltz Hesitation Step: Step forward left, swing right leg forward and past left, then lightly touch the right toe forward to the floor. The backward step is done in reverse.

Waltz Step: Step forward left, step forward right, close the left foot to the right, placing the weight on the left foot; step forward right, step forward left, close the right foot to the left, placing the weight on the right foot.

Waltz Box: Step forward left, step sideways right with right foot, close the left foot to the right, placing the weight on the left foot. The backward step is done in reverse, starting with step backward right.

Whole-Hey: See Half-Hey.

Windmills: The arms are extended out to the side, shoulders high. Keeping the arms stiff, the body is bent at the waist from side to side.

RECORD SOURCES

American Music Company, Los Angeles, California.

American Squares, 121 Delaware St., Woodbury, New Jersey.

Century Music Publishing Company, 235 W. 40th St., New York, New York.

Colorado Springs Music Company, Colorado Springs, Colorado.

Durlacher, Ed., "Honor Your Partner," three square dance albums with teaching instructions and calls on each record; Square Dance Associates, 102 North Columbus Ave., Freeport, New Jersey.

Evans, Ruth, "Childhood Rhythm Records," 326 Forest Park Avenue, Springfield, Massachusetts.

Folkraft Record Company, 7 Oliver Street, Newark, New Jersey.

Kremers, Ed., 262 O'Farrell St., No. 301, United Nations Theatre Bldg., San Francisco, California.

Morrey's Folk Art Shop, 703 Hennepin Ave., Minneapolis, Minnesota.

R.C.A. Victor Basic Record Library for Elementary Schools (Rhythms, Folk Dances, and Singing Games). For information write to Educational Services, R.C.A. Victor, Camden, New Jersey.

R.C.A. Victor Music Dealers.

Record Squares, 152 Swall Drive, Los Angeles, California.

Woodhull's "Old Tyme Masters," two albums with calls; excellent for beginning groups; R.C.A. Victor.

BIBLIOGRAPHY

Association for Supervision and Curriculum Development, *Organizing the Elementary School for Living and Learning*. Washington D. C.: National Education Assoc., 1947.

Baker, Gertrude, Florence Warnock, and Grace Christensen, *Graded Lessons in Fundamentals of Physical Education*. New York: A. S. Barnes and Co., 1938.

Barnett, Cecill, *Games, Rhythms and Dances*. Oskosh, Wisconsin: J. O. Frank and Sons, 1941.

Bertail, Inez, *Complete Nursery Song Book*. New York: Lathrop, Lee, and Shepard Co., 1947.

Bowers, Ethel, *Parties, Musical Mixers, and Simple Square Dances*. New York: National Recreation Assoc., 1937.

Burchenal, Elizabeth, *Folk Dance Series*. New York: G. Schirmer, Inc., 1929.

Cotteral, Bonnie and Donnie, *The Teaching of Stunts and Tumbling*. A. S. Barnes and Co., 1926.

Crabtree, Eunice Katherine, L. V. C. Walker, and D. Canfield, *Playtime Fun*. Lincoln, Nebraska: University Publishing Co., 1945.

Crawford, Caroline, *Dramatic Games and Dances for Little Ones*. New York, A. S. Barnes and Co., 1941.

Curtis, Mary Louise, and Adelaide B. Curtis, *Physical Education for Elementary Schools*. Milwaukee: The Bruce Publishing Co., 1945.

Duggan, Anne, Jeannette Schlottmann, and Abbie Rutledge, *The Folk Dance Library*. New York: A. S. Barnes and Co., 1948.

Education Department, *Physical Education for Elementary*

Schools. (Grades 1, 2, 3.) Baltimore: Department of Education, 1936.

Education Department, *Physical Education for Elementary Schools* (Grades 4, 5, 6). Baltimore: Department of Education, 1936.

Elsom, J. C. and Blanche Trilling, *Social Games and Group Dances.* Philadelphia: J. B. Lippincott Co., 1927.

Ford, Mr. and Mrs. Henry, *Good Morning.* Dearborn, Michigan: Dearborn Publishing Co., 1943.

Frissell, Bernice and Mary Louise Friebele, *Fun at the Playground.* New York: Macmillan Co., 1946.

Frymir, Alice, and Marjorie Hillas, *Team Sports for Women.* New York: A. S. Barnes and Co., 1942.

Gesell, A. and Frances Ilig, *The Child from Five to Ten.* New York: Harper and Brothers, 1946.

Gomez, Winifred Loerch, *Merry Songs for Boys and Girls.* New York: Follett Publishing Co., 1949.

Harris, Jane A., Anne Pittman, and Marlys Swensen, *Dance Awhile.* Minneapolis, Minnesota: Burgess Publishing Co., 1950.

Herman, Michael, *Folk Dances for All.* New York: Barnes and Noble, Inc., 1947.

Herman, Michael, *The Folk Dancer (Catalogue of Folk Dance Records and Books).* Barnes and Noble, Inc., N. Y.

Hinman, Mary Wood, *Ring Games and Dances.* New York: A. S. Barnes and Co., 1922.

Hinman, Strong, *Physical Education in Elementary Grades.* New York: Prentice Hall, 1939.

Hofer, Mary Ruef, *Children's Singing Games, Old and New.* Flanigan Co., 1914.

Horrigan, Olive K., *Creative Activities in Physical Education.* New York: A. S. Barnes and Co., 1929.

Jack, Harold K., *Physical Education for Small Elementary Schools.* New York: A. S. Barnes and Co., 1941.

Jones, Morgan, and Stevens, *Methods and Materials in Elementary Physical Education.* Yonkers-on-Hudson, New York: World Book Co., 1950.

Kirkell, Miriam, and Irma Schaffnit, *Partners All—Places All!* New York: E. P. Dutton and Co., 1949.

LaSalle, Dorothy, *Play Activities for Elementary Schools*. New York: A. S. Barnes and Co., 1934.

Manners, Zeke, *American Square Dances*. New York: Robbins Music Corp., 1948.

Meissner, Wilhelmine, and Elizabeth Meyers, *Basketball for Girls*. New York: A. S. Barnes and Co., 1940.

Muller, Al, *All American Square Dances*. New York: Paull-Pioneer Music Corp., 1948.

Murray, Arthur, *How to Become a Good Dancer*. New York: Simon and Shuster, Inc., 1947.

Neilson, N. P., and W. Van Hagen, *Physical Education for Elementary Schools*. New York: A. S. Barnes and Co., 1932.

Nicoll, James, and May Long, *Developmental Physical Education*. Yonkers-on-Hudson, New York: World Book Co., 1947.

Noren, Arthur, *Softball*. New York: A. S. Barnes and Co., 1940.

Rath, Emil, *The Folk Dance in Education*. Minneapolis, Minnesota: The Burgess Publishing Co., 1939.

Rodgers, Martin, *A Handbook of Stunts*. New York: The Macmillan Co., 1935.

Ryan, Grace, *Dances of Our Pioneers*. New York: A. S. Barnes and Co., 1939.

Salt, Benton E., Grace Fox, Elsie M. Douthett, and B. K. Stevens, *Teaching Physical Education in the Elementary School*. New York: A. S. Barnes and Co., 1942.

Shaw, Lloyd, *Cowboy Dances*. Caldwell, Idaho: Caxton Printers, 1939.

Sharp, Cecil J., *The Country Dance Book*. London, England: Novello and Company, Ltd., 1913.

Smalley, Jeannette, *Physical Education Activities for the Elementary School*. Millbrae, California: The National Press, 1950.

Staley, Seward C., *Games, Contests, and Relays*. New York: A. S. Barnes and Co., 1924.

State of New York, *Physical Education Syllabus-Elementary Schools (Book II)*. Albany: University of State of New York, 1934.

Stecher, William A., and Grover Mueller, *Games and Dances.*
    Philadelphia : Theodore Presser Co., 1941.
Victor Talking Machine Co., *Catalogue of Records.* Camden,
    New Jersey : Victor Talking Machine Co., 1948.

INDEX

277